MY
Crystal
GUIDE

MY
Crystal
GUIDE

Learn how to identify, grow, and work with crystals and discover the amazing things they can do

Philip Permutt
and Nicci Roscoe

CICO **Kidz**

We would like to dedicate this book to children all over the world to whom the future belongs. Sending much love, healing, and sparkly crystal light to you all!

Nicci and Philip xx

Published in 2021 by CICO Books
An imprint of Ryland Peters & Small Ltd
20–21 Jockey's Fields   341 E 116th St
London WC1R 4BW   New York, NY 10029

www.rylandpeters.com

10 9 8 7 6 5 4 3 2

A CIP catalog record for this book is available from the Library of Congress and the British Library.

ISBN: 978-1-80065-015-2

Printed in China

Photographer: Penny Wincer
Stylist: Nel Haynes

Commissioning editor:
Kristine Pidkameny
Senior editor: Carmel Edmonds
Senior designer: Emily Breen
Art director: Sally Powell
Production manager:
Gordana Simakovic
Publishing manager: Penny Craig
Publisher: Cindy Richards

SAFETY NOTE FOR PARENTS/CARERS AND CHILDREN

Please note that while the descriptions of the properties of crystals refer to healing benefits, they are not intended to replace diagnosis of illness or ailments, or healing or medicine. Always consult your doctor or other health professional in the case of illness. Small crystals can be a choking hazard so should never be left within reach of younger children. Some crystals can be toxic, so never make crystal water (see page 48) with a crystal unless you are certain that it is a safe nontoxic variety. Neither the authors nor the publisher can accept any responsibility or liability for any harm arising from participating in the activities described in this book.

Contents

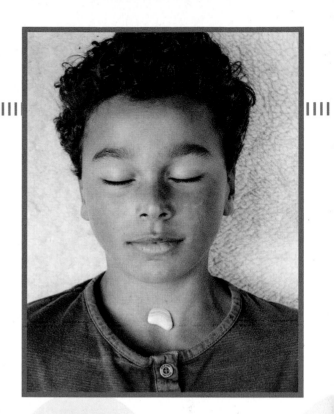

Introduction for parents and carers

We're delighted to give your children their own special book about crystals and hope you will enjoy their crystal journey with them. The following pages have lots of learning fun, including colorful pictures and different exercises to motivate children, give them confidence, and help them relax and feel calm if they're feeling anxious and worried about things, such as tests or upsets with friends. We show them how to do different meditations, including some for relaxation, which can help them sleep better at night, and some to boost confidence, which they can use before things like giving a show and tell to their class. Some of the exercises require parental guidance and we've stated wherever this will be needed. There are also exercises they can do with their friends online or in person (with suggestions for social distancing if needed).

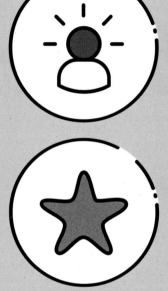

In Chapter 5, we give you a description of all the crystals we talk about and what they can do to help your children. Crystals are magical and wonderful and give so much in many ways as you'll see in this book. However, it's important to note that if your child is unwell and needs to see a doctor, we want them to know their crystals will comfort them and the doctor will give them medicine to get better. Having their crystals alongside conventional medicine, such as by their side if they have surgery, can make them feel better and speed their recovery.

Finally, Chapter 6 addresses a variety of situations where your child might need help, from dealing with change to coping at school and having more fun with their friends.

We wish you and your children a special time exploring the wonderful world of crystals and having lots of fun doing all the suggested exercises, games, and meditations.

Sending you lots of love and sparkly, happy crystal energy,

Nicci and Philip

Introduction for children

Welcome to the magical world of crystals that help you to smile, sparkle, and shine. This is a special book for you to explore and discover lots of things about crystals and how they can help you.

We take you on a wonderful journey through the magical crystal world, where every page is full of bright, colorful pictures. You'll learn about where crystals come from and how they can be powerful, just like Harry Potter's wand! And we'll teach you how to play fun games with them, as well as how to relax with them to have lovely calming feelings, especially if you're feeling anxious or worried about anything at school or with your friends.

We hope you have fun with your new crystal friends!

Sending you lots of love and sparkly, happy crystal energy,

Nicci and Philip

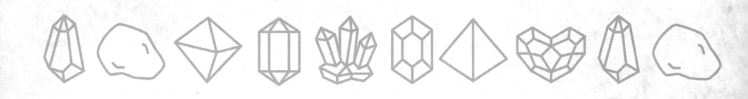

CHAPTER 1

The exciting world of science and crystals

In this chapter you will learn all about
crystals, how they are formed, where to
find them, and more.

What are crystals?

All the crystals, minerals, and rocks in the world are friends you can work with to do special things.

Stone People

Our crystal friends are alive, just like us—see opposite—and for this reason we sometimes call them Stone People.

In this book, we call all these special stones crystals, whether they are crystals, minerals, or rocks, to show that they all have special powers that can help us whenever we need them.

Minerals

A mineral is formed in space, the earth, the sea, or the sky. It's a natural material that is made of the same thing all the way through. Some minerals form crystals and some minerals form rocks, pebbles, mountains, and sand. Minerals are an amazing part of nature.

Crystals

A crystal comes in seven different perfect shapes (see page 16). All crystals are formed from minerals (and are the same type of mineral all the way through, although some may have bits of other crystals inside them, which are called inclusions), but not all minerals form crystals, because they don't have a perfect crystal shape.

Rocks

A rock may be made of different minerals in the same piece, but is not one of the seven crystal shapes.

This is shungite, which is a mineral. (This piece of shungite has been polished—see page 17.)

This is aquamarine, which is a crystal.

This is snowflake obsidian, which is a rock.

Are crystals alive?

Biologists are scientists who study living things like you and me, and plants and animals. They say that for anything to be called "living," it must be able to eat, grow, and have babies. So, are crystals living beings?

Crystals eat!

They eat the environment that they're growing in. Just like you, each crystal needs specific "foods" to grow. For example, quartz crystals eat silicon and oxygen from their surroundings, whereas selenite needs calcium, sulfur, oxygen, and hydrogen to grow.

Crystals grow!

Crystals gradually get bigger over time, even if it's such a long time that we can't see it. You can find little crystals and big crystals.

Crystals have baby crystals!

When a crystal gets separated from its crystal friends (like when a crystal is separated from a wall of a crystal cave because of an earth movement, such as a volcano exploding), it sometimes has baby crystals growing on its end. Small pieces of crystal act as seeds for the next generation too.

Earthquake quartz is a quartz crystal that was damaged by earthquakes while still in the ground but then continued growing.

How are crystals formed?

Crystals (true crystals, rather than minerals and rocks) are really special things that have all their molecules (see below) fitting together in a special pattern. All the molecules in a crystal are the same. When there are lots of these crystal molecules, they grow into the shape of the crystal you can see. We call this crystallization.

What are molecules?

Molecules are made of atoms. Both molecules and atoms are very tiny—they are so small that you can't even see them without a special microscope. When a few atoms get together in the same shape, we call them a molecule. It is like a team of atoms, with each atom playing in its own fixed position. Molecules are the building blocks of everything in the world—crystals, plants, books, toys, and even you!

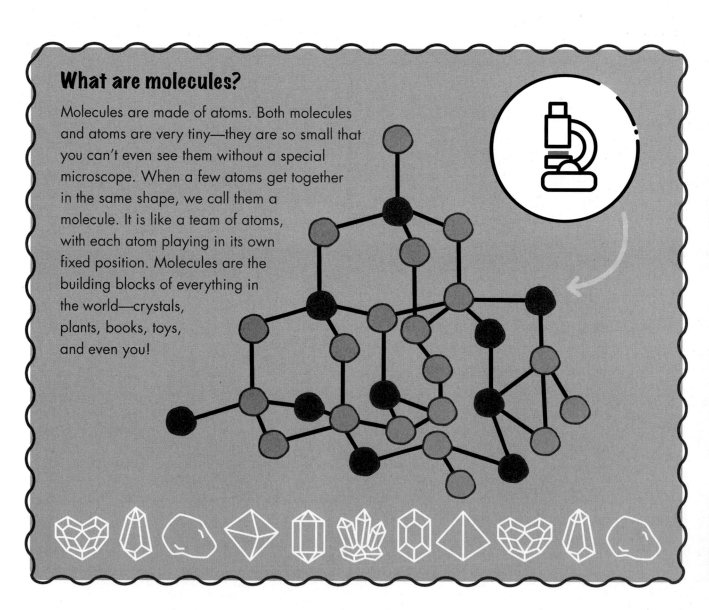

How do crystals grow?

When certain things happen to rocks, crystals can be formed in one of two ways.

Melting

Crystals grow in nature when hot liquids cool and get hard. The center of the Earth is very hot, so it heats up rocks deep underground, turning them into liquid called magma. This means the molecules of the rocks can move around. When too much pressure builds up from the heat, a bump is formed on the earth—a volcano. When this explodes, the magma becomes lava (it is still liquid rock, but it is called lava when it rises to the Earth's surface), and as it cools, the molecules come back together and form crystals.

The melted rock is called magma, which rises to the surface of the Earth as a volcano.

Dissolving

Another way crystals can grow is when you have a mixture with crystal molecules that slowly evaporates (see page 15), like salt crystals which grow in puddles of sea water as the sun dries it out and the water disappears. In nature, when rocks are in water, minerals within them can be dissolved into the water. This might be groundwater—the water between underground soil and rock—or the oceans. When the water is cooled or evaporates, the minerals can find each other and come together to form crystals. Usually it takes a very long time—many years—for crystals to grow from melted rock or rocks in water.

Grow your own crystals

It's easy to grow salt crystals. They are safe crystals that you can grow in your kitchen. Please do this exercise with an adult to help you.

YOU WILL NEED

1 cup of hot water (ask an adult to help you with this: the hot water works best if it's boiling, but it's okay if the water's very hot but not quite boiling—you may just need to stir it for longer)

¼ cup (270g) table salt

2 teaspoons white vinegar

A bit of a sponge or a rough rock

A shallow dish

1 Make your crystal growing mixture by putting the water, salt, and vinegar into a container and stir until the salt dissolves, which means you won't be able to see it in the liquid anymore.

2 Place the piece of sponge or rough rock into the shallow dish. Pour some of the salt-water mixture over the sponge, so that it almost covers the bottom of the dish and the sponge can soak up the liquid. If you're using a rough rock, then the mixture should cover the rock. Keep any of the crystal growing mixture that's left over in a sealed container.

3 Put the dish in a warm spot, like a sunny windowsill. You will see your crystals start to grow the next morning or within a day or so. Add more crystal growing mix to replace the liquid that disappears. You can carry on growing your crystals for as long as you like. They're completely safe, so you can keep your crystals and wash everything else you've used.

How do salt crystals grow?

Salt dissolves in hot water, which means the molecules of the salt move apart in the liquid. When you pour the hot mixture over the sponge or rock, the liquid starts to disappear into the air. We call this evaporation—when a liquid is heated and becomes a vapor. When this happens, the salt is concentrated—there is not so much water for the salt molecules to move around in, so they start to come together again and become crystals, or crystallize. The salt crystals grow on the sponge or rock, and sometimes they'll grow on the sides of the bowl, too. Although some crystals take a very long time to grow, these salt crystals grow quickly.

Crystal shapes

There are only seven very special shapes that make crystals look and act differently to everything else on the planet, like rocks, stones, sand, mountains, and earth. All crystals are found in one of these seven shapes.

Cubic

A cubic crystal looks like a box, and can have six, eight, or even 12 sides.

Pyrite crystals are cubic.

Trigonal

This has three sides.

Calcite crystals are trigonal. This photo shows several white calcite "dogtooth" crystals clustered together.

Hexagonal

A hexagonal crystal is a column with six sides. (Even though some hexagonal crystals have a termination (see page 102) which might look like a "side," it isn't!)

All quartz crystals are hexagonal.

Monoclinic

A monoclinic crystal looks like a strange box with lots of different sides.

Kunzite crystals are monoclinic.

Orthorhombic

This is a strange shape where three of the sides are different lengths to the other three sides. This means it can make lots of different shapes such as two pyramids stuck together or six-sided barrel-shaped crystals joined up, or even be like a squashed cube.

Aragonite crystals are orthorhombic.

Tetragonal

This looks a bit like a cube, but has one longer side.

Zircon crystals are tetragonal.

Triclinic

This can look like many different shapes put together.

Kyanite crystals are triclinic.

Natural and polished crystals

Some people polish crystals to make them pretty, shiny, and smooth when you touch them. Some polished crystals are tumble-polished, which means they are put in a barrel attached to a motor that spins the barrel round slowly. The barrel is mostly filled with rough crystals or rocks with grits and polish. Over a few weeks, this makes the crystals rounded and smooth and shiny. Other polished crystals are cut or carved into shape using special tools with diamond-toothed blades. Then they are polished to a high shine.

Natural crystals feel rougher and are not as shiny, but lots of them are still pretty. Rough or natural crystals and stones are exactly as they have come out of the ground and are just cleaned.

These crystals are both blue lace agate, but the top one has been polished and the bottom one is natural.

The life of an amethyst crystal

Some amethyst crystals (see page 80) grow in an area that started forming 2 billion years ago! Most amethyst crystals in this region are between 2 billion years and 200 million years old. Do you wonder what these crystals might have seen in their lifetime?

2 billion years ago

magma from volcanoes is cooling and crystals start to grow (see page 13).

520 million years ago

trilobites are swimming in the oceans—they were sea animals with shells that looked like very big woodlice, and they no longer exist.

200 million years ago

dinosaurs are roaming the Earth.

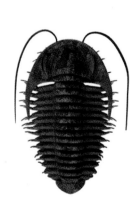

5,000 years ago

in ancient Egypt, amethyst is considered a "royal stone" and amethyst crystals (plus others such as lapis lazuli, turquoise, malachite, and quartz) are carved into statues of gods and animals and are worn to protect people from bad things. Some amethyst jewelry was found in the tomb of Tutankhamun, a boy king who lived 3,300 years ago.

1,600 years ago

in Britain, amethyst beads are placed in Anglo-Saxon graves.

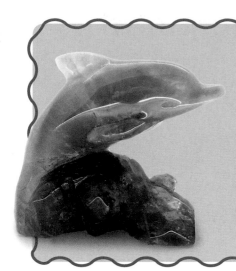

Where are amethysts now?

Amethyst is found in every crystal healer's toolbox. It can be seen on ornaments in homes, often carved into bowls, Buddhas, angels, and animals. In technology, it's used to help doctors see deeper into your body with special infrared machines.

65 million years ago

a giant rock from space, called a meteorite, hits the Earth and kills all the dinosaurs. We can still find small rocks from space, like this piece of meteorite.

3.5 million years ago

the first ancestors of you and me walk on the Earth.

200,000 years ago

people just like you and me are walking over the Earth, and some of them have probably started collecting crystals.

1,500 years ago

in Europe, soldiers carry amethyst to keep them safe in battle.

1,400 years ago

amethyst rings are worn by Catholic bishops to show how important they are in the church.

120 years ago

in 1901, amethyst jewelry is added to the Crown Jewels in the UK.

How do crystals get their names?

Crystals get their names for all sorts of reasons—from people, places, and what they look like. Sometimes we just don't know why they're called by their name, but here are a few of the ones we do know.

Ruby and opal

The names of some crystals come from ancient languages. Ruby comes from *rubeus*, which means "red" in Latin, the language the Romans spoke. Opal comes from the word *upala*, which means "jewel" in Sanskrit, an ancient Indian language.

Ruby   Blue opal

Agate and amazonite

Some crystals are named after the place they were first found. Agate was found in the Achate river (called the Dirillo today) in Sicily, Italy, and amazonite was named after the Amazon river in Brazil.

Agate   Amazonite

Howlite and angelite

Some crystals are named after the person who found them, like howlite, which is named after Henry How, who discovered it in 1868. Angelite is named after Angelica, who was the girlfriend of the person who discovered it. He was a miner—someone who finds and digs up rocks.

Howlite

Angelite

Hawk's eye

This crystal looks like the patterns in the eye of a hawk, which are created by the light effect called chatoyancy (see page 81).

Jade

This crystal gets its name because the Spanish explorers in South America saw local people holding the stone to their side, saying it cured problems with their kidneys. The Spanish explorers called it *piedra de ijada*, which means "pain in the side stone."

Kunzite

This crystal is named after George Frederick Kunz, who discovered it. He was the vice president in 1903 of Tiffany & Co in New York, which is a famous company that makes things out of crystals, like jewelry and lampshades.

Morganite

This beautiful pink crystal was called goshenite after the town of Goshen in Massachusetts where it was found. When the mineralogical society in the USA needed money, they renamed it after the banker J.P. Morgan! The colorless type is still called goshenite.

Morganite

Bloodstone

This crystal is simply named because of the red dots on it that look like drops of blood.

Goshenite

Finding crystals

Crystals are all around us if you know where to look!

Where are crystals found in nature?

In soil, in caves, and underground, as well as in the sky as snowflakes. You can find crystals on the beach, in the hills and mountains, and in caves. Always ask an adult to supervise you and never go by yourself.

And in your home?

Crystals are in watches, computers, LCDs (liquid crystal displays, which are screens in some types of television, computer, smartphone, and more), games consoles, cellphones, televisions, washing machines, and dryers, as well as jewelry and ornaments.

CRYSTAL FACTS

The largest crystals ever found are in the Cave of the Crystals in Naica, Mexico. The largest of the giant selenite crystals there is 39 feet (12 meters) long!

And the largest quartz crystal found was in Itapore, Brazil. It was 20 feet (6.1 meters) long and weighed over 88,000 pounds (almost 40,000 kilograms)!

And where else can you find crystals?

Ruby crystals in lasers—that's why they're red. And diamonds in rings, but you can also find them in some saw blades because they're the hardest natural thing on Earth!

Where can you buy crystals?

You can find crystals you can buy in lots of shops, tourist attractions, and market stalls around the world, but the best place to buy them is a specialist crystal shop or a mineral show where you will find the best quality and selection.

How rare are crystals?

You can find some crystals almost everywhere, like the quartz group of crystals which includes agates and jaspers as well as quartz crystals. Did you know that some people guess that up to 90% of the land surface of Earth might be quartz of one type or another?

Other crystals, like diamonds and rubies, are very rare and highly valued. The Pink Star Diamond, which was found in South Africa in 1999, sold for $83 million (£64.3 million) at auction. It's about the size of a big agate tumble-polished stone (see page 17) you might buy in a store for $5 (£3.50).

Other crystals are very, very rare, like painite, a red crystal. Only a very few painite crystals have ever been found.

The rarest crystals are found in only one place in the world, like tanzanite which is found only in the Merelani Hills in Tanzania, and Herkimer diamond which is from Herkimer County, New York, USA.

Herkimer diamond

Tanzanite

Crystal legends

A very long time ago, people started telling each other stories of wonderful crystals and the amazing things they did. These are stories people might tell sitting round a campfire. Here are some of the stories we've collected for you.

Opal

Opals are good for your eyes. Some people believed they would make your eyesight better and weaken your enemies' eyes, making you invisible to them! This is why opal got the nickname "stone of thieves."

One type of opal is called fire opal and has its own story. A long time ago people believed that the Storm God made storms and the Rainbow God stopped them. One day the Storm God got so angry with the Rainbow God for ending his storm that he broke the Rainbow into a thousand tiny pieces, which fell to Earth, becoming embedded in the rocks and creating fire opal.

Turquoise

Turquoise is the lucky stone of Native Americans. They believe it connects them to their god, Father Sky. He protects them on their journeys. Native Americans believe a journey can be going on holiday to a different place or even a different country, or walking to the corner store. Wherever you go, you are protected by Father Sky.

Quartz

The word crystal comes from the Greek word *krystallos*, which means "ice." When the ancient Greeks found quartz crystals in caves on their sacred mountain Olympus, they thought it was ice. When they took this "ice" out of the cave into the sun it didn't melt! They believed it was frozen by the gods so it couldn't melt in the sun. They used to say that if you held a quartz crystal when you prayed, your prayers would be granted.

Agate

In the Bible, the Hebrew priests associated crystals with animals, and agate is the stone of the lion. In another story from the Bible (and also in stories from India and southern Africa), it was said that a hair plucked from a lion's mane would give you courage. But luckily for all children in need of courage, agate is a good thing to use instead!

Fire opal

Turquoise

Quartz

Tree agate

HAPPINESS AND SUNSHINE MEDITATION

Laughing and smiling can help us feel so much better. Imagining lots of sunshine and fun times can help us laugh! Here's a crystal meditation that's full of sparkly light and happiness with orange calcite. When you put this crystal together with other happiness crystals, it can give you even more of a magical, lovely feeling.

STEP BY STEP · MEDITATION

1 Choose one of the happiness crystals to go with your orange calcite from the box to the right by using your intuition or your pendulum (see pages 35–37).

2 Sit on your sofa or upright on your bed with cushions behind you so you feel nice and comfortable. Hold the orange calcite in one hand and the other crystal you have chosen in your other hand.

Crystals for happiness

Citrine

Rose quartz

Rhodochrosite

Rainbow moonstone

Dalmatian stone

3 Close your eyes and take a slow, deep breath in through your nose as you count to 4 in your head. Then slowly breathe out through your mouth, counting to 5 in your head. Repeat this three times.

4 Now breathe normally. Imagine a time you had lots of fun and laughed with your friends or your family. Maybe you were on vacation on the beach and having fun swimming in the sea and playing in the sand.

5 Squeeze your crystals in your hands and imagine yourself having fun and feeling happy. Imagine stepping into the picture you see and hear the sounds of the waves splashing and feel the lovely, warm, sparkly sun on your face. See yourself playing games on the beach with your family and/or friends. As you look up and see the bright blue sky and the sparkly sun shining down, you know everything will be okay and you feel so much happier and start to laugh and smile even more. Enjoy being in this lovely place while you're squeezing your orange calcite and other crystal.

6 Take three deep breaths slowly in through your nose and out through your mouth, and when you're ready open your eyes.

7 Every time you want to feel sunshine and happiness on days that you want to feel better, just imagine squeezing your orange calcite and other crystal (or if you have your crystals with you, hold them) and imagine yourself back in this special place on the beach having fun in the sparkly sunshine.

Orange calcite

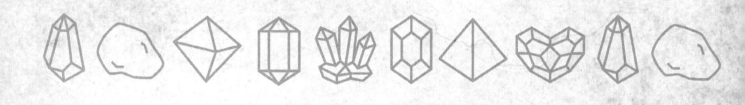

CHAPTER 2

The magical energy of your crystals

Did you know that crystals have special powers? Here you will discover the amazing things that crystals can do.

Crystal energy

Everything has energy, from the biggest animal, such as an elephant, to even the smallest little crystal, and crystals love energy. All these things that crystals can do help them to heal things and give energy.

What can crystals do with energy?

• They can focus energy—like the way a ruby that is in a laser directs a laser beam far away.

• They can store energy, like computers store information and send it, as quartz does with light (see opposite).

• They can change energy from one type to another—for example, quartz crystals in watches change electricity into a movement that vibrates and keeps the time correctly.

Feeling crystal energy

Try this exercise with a friend to feel it for yourself. You will need a quartz crystal with a point.

1 Hold both your hands out in front of you with your palms up, and close your eyes.

2 Ask your friend to hold the quartz crystal just above one of your hands with the point pointing to your hand without touching it, and move it slowly in a circle round and round lots of times.

3 How do your hands feel? Do they feel different from one another? Can you feel heat or cold in one hand, or maybe it feels tingly, heavy, or light? Anything you feel is okay—even if you feel something you don't understand or don't have words for, you can just call it your "crystal feeling."

4 Swap with your friend and repeat this so they can feel their crystal feeling too.

This is titanium quartz, which can help you feel crystal energy.

Your energy body

Your physical body is made up of your head, chest, tummy, arms, and legs, but you have an "energy body" too, made up of your chakras, meridians, and aura.

Your aura

The aura is an energy field that is around every living thing. Everything you feel comes through your aura before it can touch you. You can imagine it as a shining light around you, like a spark of magical light from Harry Potter's wand. This light comes out of your chakras and helps to keep you safe and well. Some crystals can boost your aura when you hold them, making your aura bigger and stronger, which keeps you even safer. Some people can see the aura around you like a hazy glow. You can feel someone's aura if you put your hand close to them without touching. Try it with your friends or parents.

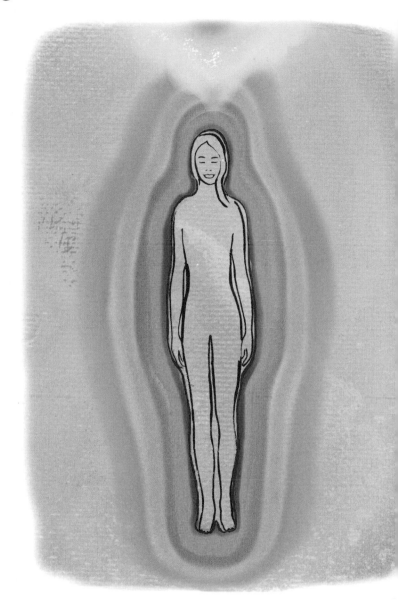

Carry these crystals to boost your aura

| Amazonite | Amethyst | Black tourmaline | Aqua aura |

Chakras and meridians

Imagine a colored water flowing through little pathways in your body.

Where these pathways cross or meet up there's a small pool of colored water. The colored water represents energy. The pathways are called meridians, and the pools are called chakras. *Chakra* is a word that comes from India and means "wheel" or "circle" in Sanskrit, an old Indian language.

Chakras are like doorways for energy. When we heal ourselves or our friends, we can put crystals on the chakras so the energy can easily go through the doorways to help them feel better.

The chakras are often called hotspots because there's more energy where they are, so it's easier for your body to use the energy. Sometimes the chakras can really feel hot when you put crystals on them!

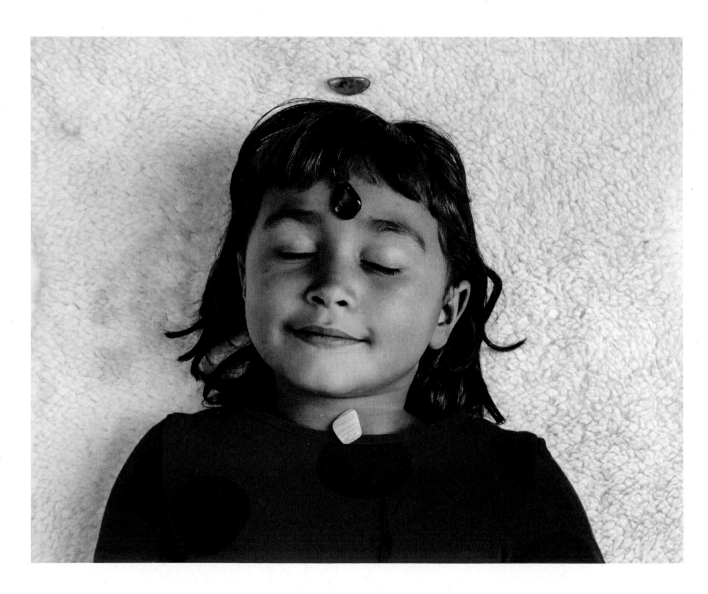

Where are the chakras?

There are seven chakras on our body in special places. Here's a picture showing you where they are.

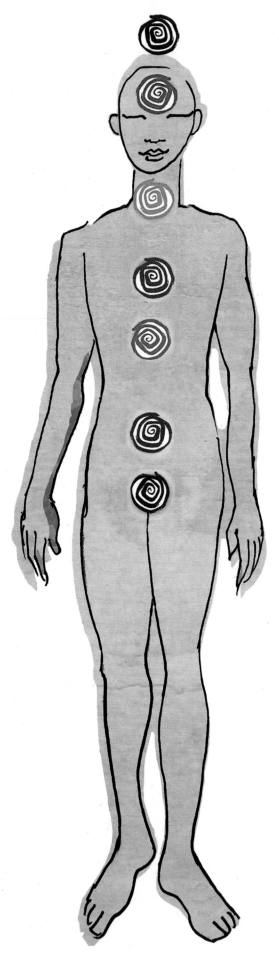

 CROWN
top of your head

 BROW
middle of your forehead
(sometimes called the third eye)

 THROAT
bottom of your throat

 HEART
center of your chest

 SOLAR PLEXUS
just below your heart

 SACRAL
just below your belly button

 BASE
a bit further down from your belly button

Crystals and chakras

Just like you, your chakras can be happy or sad, healthy or unwell. Putting the right crystals on them will make you feel better and keep you well when you are feeling good too. (See also pages 64–65.) These special crystals work especially well with each chakra.

CROWN
amethyst

BROW
lapis lazuli

THROAT
blue lace agate

HEART
green aventurine

SOLAR PLEXUS
citrine

SACRAL
carnelian

BASE
red jasper

Alternative chakra crystals

If you can't get the crystals listed left, you can work with these crystals instead.

CROWN
quartz

BROW
sodalite

THROAT
blue chalcedony

HEART
rose quartz

SOLAR PLEXUS
yellow jasper

SACRAL
orange calcite

BASE
hematite

Choosing crystals

One of the many exciting things about crystals is deciding which ones you would like to work with.

Choosing with your intuition

If you're out with your family for lunch and they ask if you'd like pizza or chicken and salad, what is the first thing you feel and think? Do you know what you want, or do you let someone choose for you? When you wake up in the morning, do you sometimes know what you want to wear that day—maybe a white t-shirt and tracksuit bottoms, or a yellow top with jeans? This is called intuition—it's something we feel inside that tells us what we want, whether or not to do something, or if something's good or bad.

When you're choosing a crystal, you may like one you see because you love the color or the feel of it. Sometimes you might not even know why you like a crystal. This is your intuition helping you choose.

Sometimes you may see a crystal you don't like, or your pendulum (see pages 36–37) might choose it for you. Crystals like these can also really help you. So make sure you hold them and keep them with you just like the ones you do love. Your intuition helps you to notice the things you need, so sometimes you may really like them and other times you won't.

Choosing with a pendulum

You can also choose your crystal using another crystal hanging at the end of a chain, which is known as a pendulum. Thousands of years ago, cave people needed to find water, and they used special sticks called dowsing sticks to help them. They held the stick out in front of them and walked along until the stick moved up or down, which showed them where water was underground. Everyone can do this with a little practice. All the dowsing stick does is show you what your intuition tells you. Pendulums do the same thing, making it easier for you to choose the right crystals.

1 Choose a pendulum that you like and you feel comfortable with. You can buy pendulums from crystal shops, or you can even make your own by tying a crystal to a string. You need to tie it very tightly so it won't fall off, so ask an adult to help you.

2 Hold the top of the chain in your left or right hand and let the pendulum hang down. Use your other hand to keep the chain and crystal still and then take this hand away.

3 Now ask it a question to which you know the answer is "yes," such as, "Is the moon made of rock?" The pendulum will show you the answer by going round in a circle, moving backward and forward, or swinging sideways. Whichever way the pendulum goes, this is your "yes" answer when you ask it questions.

4 Stop the pendulum moving again and then ask a question to which you know the answer is "no," such as, "Is the moon made of cheese?" The pendulum will then show you the answer "no" by moving in a different way to how it answered "yes," going round in a circle, backward and forward, or sideways. Whichever

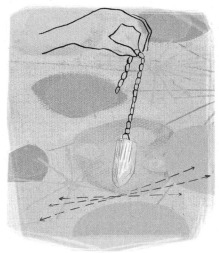

Swinging backward and forward

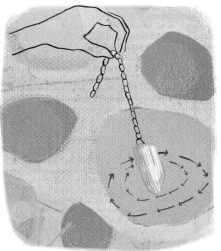

Swinging round in a circle

way the pendulum goes, this is your "no" when you ask it questions. This pendulum moves in a special way just for you. Other people's pendulums may have different ways of answering "yes" and "no." Your friend's pendulum may go round for "no," and yours may go backward and forward. This doesn't mean one of you is wrong. You are both right.

5 Now you can choose a crystal with your pendulum. Hold your pendulum in one hand and a crystal in your other hand, or put the crystal on the table. Hold your pendulum over the crystal and ask your pendulum if it is a good crystal for you to have today. If your pendulum tells you "yes," then that is the crystal for you. If it tells you "no," then keep holding your pendulum over crystals and asking the same question until you find the one for you.

Stick the chakra on the yogi

STEP BY STEP · ACTIVITY

This is a fun game to play on your own or with your friends when you are learning about chakras.

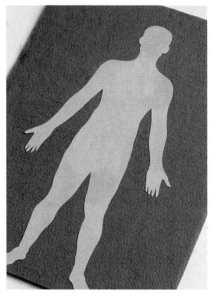

YOU WILL NEED

Paper chakra body template (see Step 1)

Scissors

A3 piece of felt

Sheets of felt in red, orange, yellow, green, light blue, dark blue, and violet

Blue tack

1 Copy the chakra body template on page 126 onto paper and cut it out. Ask an adult to help you cut out circles where the chakras are. Place or stick the picture on the A3 piece of felt.

2 Ask an adult to help you cut out circles in the special chakra rainbow colors from each of the pieces of colored felt: red for the base, orange for the sacral, yellow for the solar plexus, green for the heart, light blue for the throat, dark blue for the brow, and violet for the crown. Put a small piece of blue tack on the back of each circle.

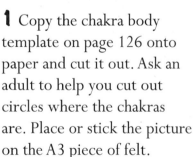

3 Now, stick the felt circles on the holes that show where the chakras are. Can you remember which circle goes where? (Remember that the crown chakra is above the head!) When you've done this yourself, try it as a game with your friends. Take off the felt chakra circles, mix them up, and let your friends guess where each colored felt chakra goes!

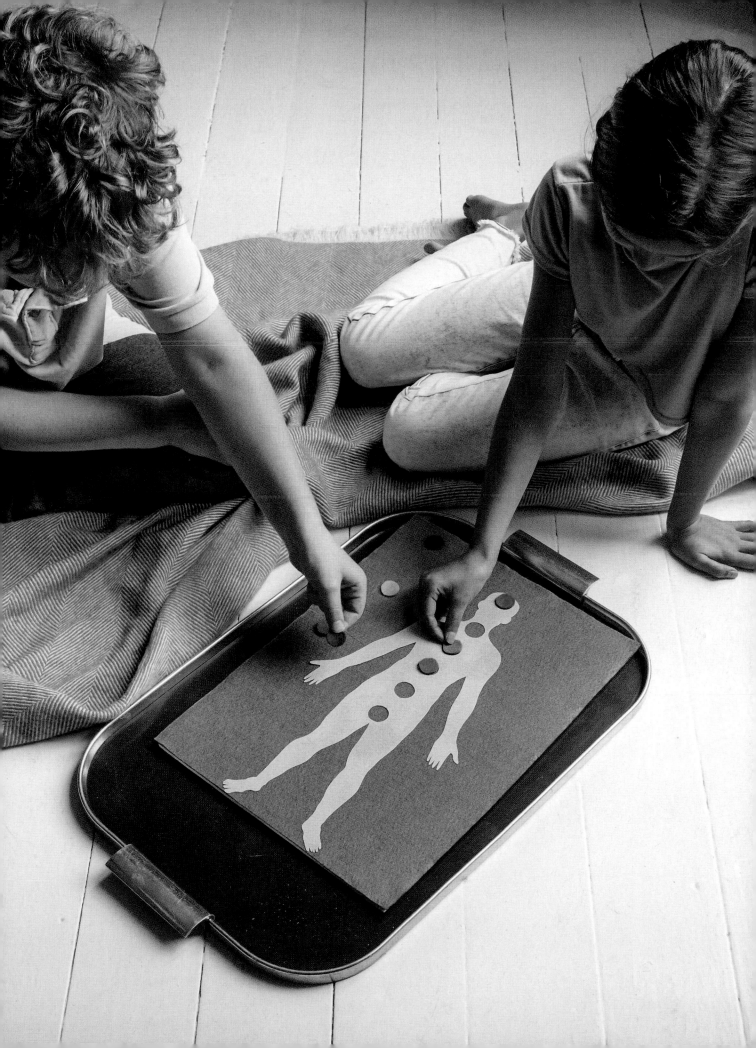

Caring for your crystals

Imagine that you have a hamster as a pet at home (or you might not need to imagine if you already have one!). It would be important to look after your hamster by regularly giving it fresh water and changing its straw and bedding to keep it well and full of energy. In the same way, you need to look after your crystals. Crystals are full of energy and light, and if you take care of them, they will shine brightly for you and give you what you need.

Cleansing your crystals

If your crystals aren't sparkly and shiny and they don't feel the same as they usually do, it means they need cleansing to give them back their full energy and light. Cleansing is different from cleaning. Cleaning washes off dirt—we clean our shoes to get the mud off them. Cleansing washes away sad or unhappy energy—like energetic "mud."

If you've been feeling upset and holding your crystals lots to help you feel better, they can hold on to the sad energy you have been feeling. By cleansing them, you will be taking this away and giving them a new, happy, positive energy, with which they can help you again.

How to cleanse your crystals

There are different ways to cleanse your crystals so they stay sparkly, shiny, and happy.

Water and soap

Crystals love bubbles! You can hear them having fun! Give them a regular bubble bath with washing-up liquid or your favorite bubble bath, and then wash them with clean, fresh water and dry them. Crystals also love fresh running

These crystals cannot be put into water because it will hurt them:

Selenite

Orange selenite

Peacock ore

Celestite

water. Put them into a bowl and let the cool/warm water run over them for about 15 minutes once a week or more if you think they need it. However, there are some crystals you can't put in water (see box on the left), so they will need to be cleansed in a different way.

Sunshine and moonlight

Every time the sun or moon comes out, crystals love having this beautiful light on them to give them lots of energy. Some crystals, such as amethyst, might fade to a lighter color in bright sunlight, so it is better to cleanse them in moonlight (or another way). Never put a crystal ball in sunlight, as it can cause a fire with the brightness of the light on it.

Burying in the earth

Crystals can be born lots of times! If you bury them in the earth for 24 hours and then take them out and wash them with clean water, they will love it! If you live in an apartment or flat, you can also fill a bowl with soil and bury them in there. (If you have a dog, this may not be a good method for you, as the dog might dig up the crystals!)

Tibetan bells or cymbals

Tibetan bells or cymbals, which are sometimes called tingsha, can also cleanse your crystals. When you ping them together over your crystals, they make a wonderful vibration as the sound bounces through them, which cleanses the energy. You can use them to cleanse your room and your house, too.

Talk to your crystal friends

Talking to your crystals and smiling at them all, just like you talk to your other friends, helps keep your little stone friends happy and bright. If you listen to your intuition (see page 35), you will hear or feel your crystals talking to you and they will tell you what you need. The more time you spend with your crystals and talk to them, the more they'll give you to help you feel so much better. Crystals love it when you talk to them!

Keeping your crystals safe

Some crystals can get broken if they're dropped or if they bang together, so here are some ways to try to keep them safe.

• At home, you can put your different crystals anywhere in your room, such as on a bookshelf or your nightstand, and you can keep some of them on your windowsill so they enjoy the light and sunlight shining on to them (but don't keep a crystal ball there—see page 41). You can also put tumble-polished stones (see page 17) together in bowls in your room too. Be careful if you have pets that your crystals aren't somewhere that the animals could reach them or knock them on to the floor. If you have lots of small crystals, you can put them in a box that has other little box sections inside it, to keep your different types of crystal apart.

• When you take a crystal to school or a friend's house, keep it safe in your pocket or schoolbag. If you take a few crystals, put them in a soft small bag or wrap them in a cloth to stop them knocking against each other. To take even more care of your favorite crystals, you can wrap them in bubble wrap or newspaper.

STEP BY STEP · MEDITATION

"SAY WHAT YOU FEEL" MEDITATION

If you feel shy or scared when you need to say something in front of anyone, like speaking in front of your class or talking to adults, blue lace agate can help you. Read through the whole meditation before starting so that you can do it lying down, or ask someone to read it to you while you're doing it.

1 Lie down on the sofa, your bed, or the floor and put your blue lace agate crystal on your throat. Lay your arms down by your sides and close your eyes.

2 Take a slow, deep breath in through your nose as you count to 4 in your head, then breathe out slowly through your mouth as you count to 5 in your head. Repeat this three times.

3 Keep your eyes closed and start breathing normally.

4 Relax your face and let your forehead soften. Feel your eyes softening at the edges and relax your cheekbones by letting go of anything that feels tight or tense in your face. Then feel your throat and the back of your neck relax, too.

5 Relax your chest and your tummy, then relax all the way down to your feet and your toes.

6 Imagine you have roots at the bottom of your feet and these are going deep into the ground, like the roots from the trees. Now imagine the roots are attaching themselves to a beautiful golden crystal ball which has everything inside it that you want to say to everyone, and has a bright, sparkly golden calcite crystal light inside that is full of confidence.

7 This beautiful golden calcite crystal light now starts to travel up through your toes, your feet, your legs, and your tummy, and you begin to feel even more relaxed.

Golden calcite

Blue lace agate

8 The light now starts to travel up to your neck and throat, and you feel your throat relax and open up as the lump leaves your throat and comes out through your neck and anywhere else in your body you feel it go.

9 The light now travels up through your head and spills out of the top, like a golden shower surrounding you. This feels warm and comforting.

10 Stay lying down and relaxing for another 5–10 minutes, to let the golden calcite crystal light work its magic.

11 When you're ready, take the blue lace agate crystal off your throat. Keep it with you during the day, and whenever you find you have difficulty finding the right words to express yourself, just hold your crystal and give it a squeeze. You can also sleep with it under your pillow or keep it on your nightstand so it can help you in your dreams while you sleep.

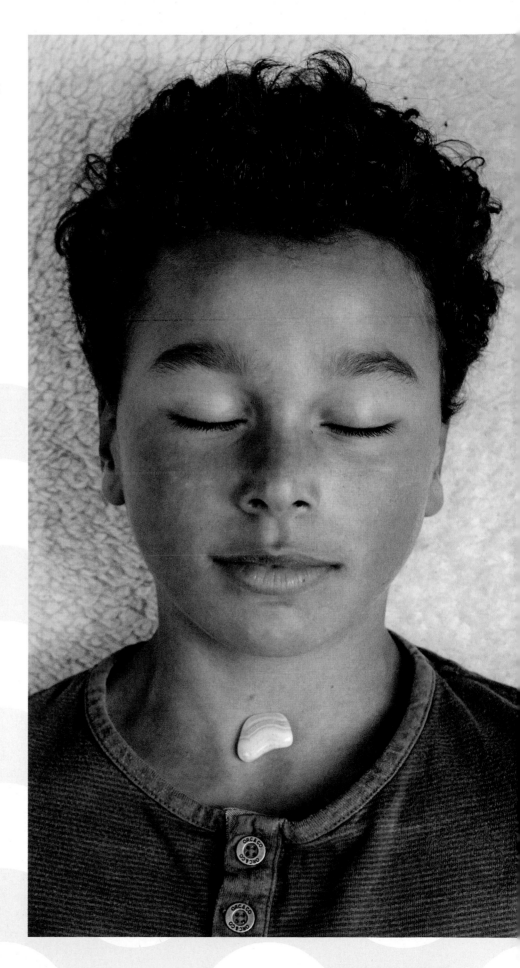

CHAPTER 3

Working with your crystals

There are all sorts of things that you can do
with your crystals, and this chapter gives
you lots of ideas.

Magical washing water

When you put a crystal into water, the special energy that it has goes into the water. You can then use this only for washing your skin or your hair—do not drink the water. This is an easy and fun way that your crystal friends can help you.

Be careful

Only use crystals for crystal washing water that we have shown you in this book. Some crystals do not like water (see page 41) and some crystals cannot be used for washing water because it would make you sick. If you are ever unsure about what type of crystal you have, do not make crystal washing water with it.

Making crystal washing water

1 Place your crystal in a bowl or jug of water and cover the bowl or jug so nothing else can fall in. Leave it overnight where no one else will touch it. This gives time for the crystal energy to come out of the crystal into the water.

2 In the morning, take the crystal out of the water and use the crystal washing water as described in Chapter 5.

3 Give the crystal a quick rinse with fresh water to cleanse it (see page 40), then it'll be ready to make another batch of crystal washing water.

Crystals and meditation

We know that crystals can help focus special energy, but did you know they can also help you meditate? When you sit quietly with your crystals, amazing things can happen in your mind, making you feel calmer, happier, and stronger.

What is meditation?

Meditation can help us feel more relaxed and give us more energy. We learn to focus on clearing our mind from worrying thoughts and chatterboxes in our head and start by sitting or lying down in a quiet, comfortable place. When we meditate with crystals we can let these thoughts flow away, and keep coming back to focus on our crystal and lovely things like stars and positive words. Everyone can do this—and it is great for grown-ups, too!

Crystals to feel calmer, happier, and so much better

Calcite

Amethyst

Falcon's eye

Harlequin quartz

Rose quartz

Green tourmaline

Tiger's eye

Celestite

Chrysoprase

Rhodonite

Labradorite

Black tourmaline

Breathe out your worries

This meditation helps you say goodbye to your worries and anxious feelings, whether you have a funny tummy, lots of thoughts are running through your head, you're not sure which group of friends you want to be in, or you can't focus on your schoolwork.

1 Choose your crystals from the crystal list in the box on page 49 by asking your pendulum (see pages 36–37) and feeling which one you are drawn to (see page 35). Maybe the color pops out at you, you like the feel of it, or you find it calming.

2 Find a comfortable place to sit and put your crystal in front of you to look at.

3 Keep looking at your crystal. Let all the worries in your head just float away. Every time any little chatterbox or worry comes into your head, just focus on your crystal.

4 Keep looking at your crystal as you take a slow, deep breath in through your nose while counting to 4 in your head. Then slowly breathe out through your mouth as you count to 5 in your head. Repeat this three times.

5 Now close your eyes and breathe normally, and imagine seeing the color of your crystal. See how much better you feel. When you feel like you are ready, open your eyes.

A morning crystal meditation

When you are worried or anxious, the good news is you can choose what you think, and you can be more in control of your feelings—which is how this meditation will help you.

1 Choose two of the crystals from the box on page 49: choose one that you feel is calming and one that you feel is positive. If you're not sure, let your pendulum help you (see pages 36–37).

2 When you wake up in the morning, before you get out of bed, sit up comfortably and hold your two chosen crystals, one in each hand.

3 Take a slow, deep breath in through your nose as you count to 4 in your head. Then slowly breathe out through your mouth, counting to 5 in your head. Repeat this three times. Now breathe normally.

4 Say the following words to yourself: "I'm feeling positive, calm, and relaxed. And I feel so much better." Say them over and over again for 2 minutes (see note below), and imagine the words are going into the crystals. If anything else comes into your head, just allow it to flow out and keep coming back to these positive words.

5 Keep the crystals with you all day, and any time you feel worried or anxious, hold your crystals or imagine them to help you feel calm, relaxed, and positive.

You can do this meditation every day and slowly build up the time spent in Step 4 saying the words to 5 minutes, then 7 minutes, and finally 10 minutes at a time. It may be helpful to keep a clock or timer nearby to help you measure the time.

SBIS: a word to make you feel better

SBIS is a special word that has a different meaning for each letter. You can use it any time you want to feel better about something that is worrying you. It helps you remember four ways to feel more positive and happier in less than a minute.

is for STOP: If a thought comes into your mind that upsets you and you are with your friends, shout "STOP" in your head so no one else hears you. If you're on your own, you could shout "STOP" out loud.

is for BREATHE: Take a deep breath in through your nose and slowly out through your mouth.

is for IMAGINE: Imagine holding your favorite crystal that helps you to feel calm and relaxed, such as rose quartz or green or blue calcite.

is for SMILE: Smile because you feel so much better!

Top to bottom: rose quartz, green calcite, and blue calcite.

Mindfulness

Mindfulness is about noticing your different emotions and what you feel, think, see, hear, smell, and taste. When you're being mindful, you may notice your chest feels tight or you have a pain in your tummy when you are anxious, upset, or worried. You may realize you can hear yourself saying negative things in your mind, like when you're worrying about what your friends think or if you'll sound okay when you stand up to speak in class.

The good news is that once you've noticed these negative thoughts, you can change them to be more positive. There are lots of mindfulness exercises you can do using your crystals, such as the breathing exercise (page 50), meditation (page 49), or affirmations (page 56), that will help you when you notice these feelings and make them better.

Not only can being mindful help you feel better if you've not been having a nice time, but it can also help you focus on things like your schoolwork, sports, art, and music.

A crystal of confidence meditation

To help us feel confident, we can try something called anchoring. Anchoring helps us think of a good memory and bring back the happy feelings we had then. We can do this by linking the memory to a special crystal. Stepping into the character of someone that we love also gives us confidence.

Crystals to feel confident

Citrine

Moonstone

Bronzite

Strawberry aventurine

Tourmaline

Jade

Rose quartz

Orange calcite

Sugilite

Crazy lace agate

1 Choose your crystal of confidence from the box opposite and hold it in your hand.

2 Take a slow, deep breath in through your nose as you count to 4 in your head. Then slowly breathe out through your mouth, counting to 5 in your head. Repeat this three times. Now breathe normally.

3 Remember a time that you were happy and confident and felt really good, and think about it for a few moments.

4 Now imagine stepping into the shoes of someone who makes you smile and laugh from a movie or book, such as Harry Potter or his friend Hermione, Anna or Elsa from *Frozen*, Moana, Paddington Bear, or Mary Poppins. Think about how good they're feeling. Imagine seeing what they're seeing and hearing how confident they are when they speak.

5 Every time you want to feel like this, hold your crystal of confidence or imagine you're holding it if you haven't got it with you.

Confident words meditation

1 Find somewhere quiet to sit by yourself, or if you want you can do this meditation with someone in your family or with your friends.

2 Hold your crystal of confidence.

3 Take a slow, deep breath in through your nose as you count to 4 in your head. Then slowly breathe out through your mouth, counting to 5 in your head. Repeat this three times. Now breathe normally.

4 Say the following words to yourself:

"I feel confident, I feel happy, and I believe in myself and what I can do."

Repeat them over and over again for 2 minutes (see page 52). If anything else comes into your mind, keep coming back to these positive words.

5 Any time you want to feel like this, hold your crystal of confidence or imagine you're holding it if you haven't got it with you.

STEP BY STEP · ACTIVITY

Positive affirmations with crystals

Affirmations are positive words that you can say to yourself while holding your crystal. This will help you to change negative thoughts like "I can't do this" to "I can do this," or "I'm so worried" to "It's going to be okay." The more you say your positive affirmations, the sooner you can start to feel better.

Using crystal affirmations

1 Choose the affirmation that you need right now from the opposite page. Take the crystal that matches the words and carry it with you in your schoolbag and hold it when you need to. Keep it on your nightstand or under your pillow at night.

2 Repeat the affirmation to yourself eight times while holding the crystal whenever you need to, no matter what time of day. Say the words to yourself before you go to sleep, too.

When you feel better, there may be another affirmation you want to choose. Do the same with these words and this crystal as you did with the first one. You can do this with as many affirmations as you want to.

Your crystal affirmations

"I can do it"
quartz

"I feel happy"
citrine

"I want to, I can, and I am going to do it"
garnet

"I believe in myself"
amethyst

"I'm confident"
crazy lace agate

"I'm calm and relaxed"
calcite

"I love myself"
rose quartz

"I can concentrate and focus"
fluorite

"I'm going to do my best"
agate

"I'm in control"
falcon's eye

"I have courage"
tiger's eye

"I feel strong"
hematite

"It's going to be okay"
tourmaline

Keeping a crystal diary

When you hold different crystals, you get particular feelings—like when you're anxious and you hold a blue calcite crystal and it calms you and makes you feel better. Some people have different feelings with the same crystal. This is normal. No one is wrong, it's just that we're all different. For example, if two different people hold a rose quartz, one may feel it's warm and the other may say it feels cool. Keeping a crystal diary is a good way to remember how you feel with each crystal each time you hold it.

YOU WILL NEED

A ruler

A pen or pencil

A notebook or exercise book

1 With your ruler and pen or pencil, copy the table shown opposite into your notebook or exercise book by drawing three lines down the page and adding the headings "day," "date," "type of crystal," and "how I feel" at the top of the four columns.

2 For the first entry, write the day and date in the first two columns. (We write the day as well as the date because the day of the week is sometimes very important. If the same feelings come up every Monday, there might be a reason for it.)

3 Now's the best bit! Take one of your crystals and hold it in your hand. Sit or stand still, close your eyes, and be quiet. Notice what you feel in your hand. Does the crystal feel heavy or light? Warm or cool? Do you get tingles like pins and needles in your hand or arm? Can you feel anything in your other hand? Do your hands feel different from each other or do they feel the same? Do you feel anything anywhere else, like your head, tummy, feet, or toes?

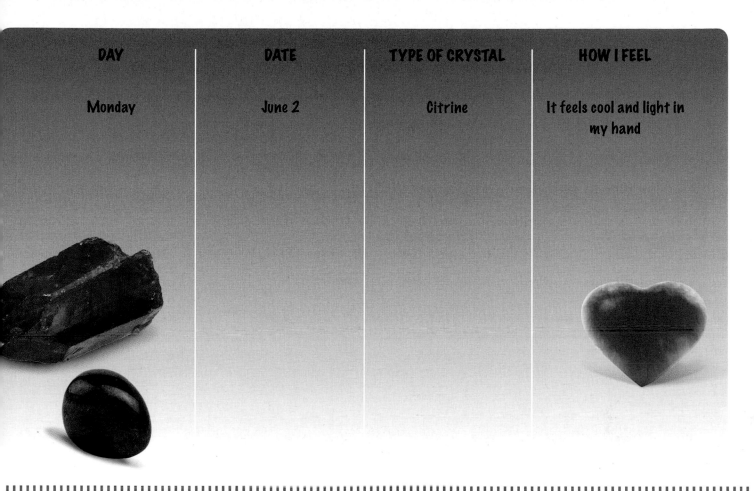

DAY	DATE	TYPE OF CRYSTAL	HOW I FEEL
Monday	June 2	Citrine	It feels cool and light in my hand

4 Write down the name of the crystal in the third column and whatever you felt when you held the crystal in the fourth column. If you don't know the name of the crystal, just write the color and shape so you'll remember which one it is.

5 Try to do this with one crystal each day. Then you will build up your own special big book of crystal knowledge. This is exactly what we did when we started working with crystals many years ago.

6 Keep doing this until your book is full. Then find another notebook or exercise book and do it all again.

Other ways to work with your crystals

There are many ways to work with your crystals by yourself. You can also look at Chapter 6 for ideas.

• Keep your crystals with you in your pocket or your schoolbag and take them out and hold them during the day.

• Wear crystal jewelry, such as crystal bracelets and necklaces, with crystals to give you what you need. Try rose quartz for love and calmness, amethyst to help with anxiety and worry, or tiger's eye to give you courage and make you feel strong from the inside out.

• Keep your crystals next to your bed at night. You can even put the crystal or crystals you need under your pillow, or hold one or two at a time. If they've disappeared in the morning, you'll find them somewhere in your bed!

• Hold a crystal that your pendulum (see pages 36–37) or you have chosen.

• Put your crystals on your chakras (see page 33).

SLEEP WELL MEDITATION WITH BLUE CALCITE

Sometimes you may go to bed and find it difficult to sleep because you have lots of things going round in your head and you just want them to go away. Here's a lovely relaxation meditation with a blue calcite crystal to help you have a very calm night's sleep without any chatterboxes in your head keeping you awake!

1 Hold your blue calcite crystal in one hand. Now lie on your bed and relax your arms down by your sides and close your eyes.

2 Take a slow, deep breath in through your nose as you count to 4 in your head, then slowly breathe out through your mouth as you count to 5 in your head. Repeat three times.

3 Keep your eyes closed and start breathing normally.

4 Imagine lots of bright golden stars around you and keep squeezing your blue calcite crystal. As you're doing this, remember all the different things you've been thinking about that have been going round and round in your head, like "Is my homework good enough?" or "What friends will I play with tomorrow?"

5 Now imagine dropping each thing you've been thinking about into one of the bright golden stars, one at a time. See each star come closer to you and let one of your thoughts float out of your head into it. Then see the star fly away until it disappears, and put your next thought into another star and see it fly away, too. Do this with all your thoughts until they're all in their own star and all the things you have been thinking have floated out of your head.

6 Squeeze your blue calcite crystal with your eyes still closed, and imagine seeing one big, beautiful star shining brightly above you and around you with sparkly bits everywhere.

7 Now feel how sleepy and relaxed you are while you think lovely calm thoughts and fall asleep holding your blue calcite crystal and having your beautiful sparkly star around you.

Blue calcite

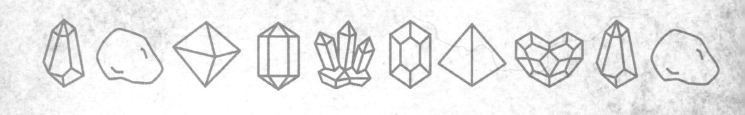

CHAPTER 4

Sharing your crystals

It's great to show your friends and family
how brilliant your crystals are! Here you
will find out how you can help the people
you care about feel better and happier.

Crystal healing

Amethyst (violet) is for the crown chakra, which is at the top of your head

Lapis lazuli (dark blue) is for the brow chakra, which is just above your eyebrows in the middle of your forehead

Blue lace agate (light blue) is for the throat chakra at the bottom of your throat

Green aventurine (green) is for the heart chakra in the middle of your chest

Citrine (yellow) is for the solar plexus chakra just below your ribcage

Carnelian (orange) is for the sacral chakra just below your belly button

Red jasper (red) is for the base chakra on the bottom of your tummy

Crystals have a beautiful energy. It's lovely to share this with your friends at any time. If a friend of yours feels worried or anxious, it can really help them feel better and calmer again.

One way to do this is with a crystal chakra set and a quartz master crystal. A quartz master crystal is a special big quartz crystal that can help make other crystals more powerful.

On the left are the crystals for your crystal chakra set that we learned about in Chapter 2. They are placed on different areas going down the center of your body, from the top of your head to the bottom of your tummy (see page 34, where you will also find the alternative crystal chakra set).

A quartz master crystal

Crystal chakra healing

1 Ask your friend to lie down somewhere comfortable. Tell them what you're going to do with the crystals which will help them relax. You're going to be gently putting each crystal on them in a different place from the top of their head to the bottom of their tummy, and then you'll be moving your quartz master crystal in a clockwise circle above each one. After this, they will keep lying there for about 2–5 minutes with the crystals on their body before you take them off. Have a clock or timer nearby if you need help measuring the time.

2 Before you start putting crystals on your friend, take one slow, deep breath in through your nose and out through your mouth, so you feel calm, relaxed, and ready to begin. Then place the crystals on your friend's chakras (see opposite) one at a time, from the base all the way up to the crown.

3 Hold your quartz master crystal with the pointy end (called the termination) pointing down toward the amethyst crystal on your friend's crown chakra. Slowly move it in clockwise circles over the amethyst. Keep doing this slowly until you feel a change in the energy of your quartz master crystal in your hand—it might start to feel warm, cold, or tingly, or get heavy or very light.

4 Repeat Step 3 for each of the other six crystals.

5 When you've done all this, sit quietly for 2–5 minutes while the crystals are still on your friend. This will help your friend feel calm, relaxed, and happy.

6 Carefully take the crystals off your friend and place them in your crystal bag or bowl. Let your friend get up when they're ready. If you want to, you can swap over and they can share crystal healing energy with you in the same way.

If you cannot be with your friend or you have to be socially distanced from them, you can tell your friend where to place the crystals on their body. While doing this you can speak to your friend on the phone or see them on a video call if you are not in the same room.

Healing yourself

If you're worried, anxious, or not feeling well, you can put a crystal chakra set on your own chakras. Have your crystals nearby so that you can put them in the right places while you're lying down.

Starting a crystal club

A crystal club is a great idea. It's a safe place where you can share what you know about your crystals and learn about your friends' crystals, too. You can ask a teacher at school if they would like to organize this, or you can ask your parents if you can invite your friends over to have a crystal club at your home. Here are a few ideas for things to do in your crystal club.

Show and tell

You or one of your friends can bring a crystal from their collection that they know something about and show it to all of you in the club. They can tell everyone what they know about it.

Share crystal healing energy

You can share crystal healing energy (see pages 64–65) with your friends in the crystal club. Lots of you can do this at the same time in pairs.

Crystal swaps

You can swap crystals with your friends. This is a really good idea if you have a few of the same type of crystal and you don't need them all right now, and they have something different that you haven't got in your collection.

Identify crystals

You can bring in crystals that you don't know the names of and see if you can work out which ones they are with your friends in the club (see Your Crystal Finder on page 76).

Organize your crystals

You can help each other to organize your crystals into different groups, like ones connected to each chakra (you can find this out in Your Crystal Finder on page 76), crystal shapes (see page 16), or colors.

Crystals at home

Your home also needs healing sometimes with love and beautiful energy so it feels calmer and a lovely, happy space to be. For example, if you've had an argument with any of your family, or they have been arguing or are upset, your crystals can help. By putting them in different places in your home, they will help heal the upsetting energy and make it feel better again.

CRYSTAL FUN AT HOME

To help you understand and talk to your pets, hold angelite or put it in your pocket when you're with your pets, and keep it with you all day, too. You can be like Dr Dolittle!

If you have a garden or yard, put rose quartz around the edges to give it love. If you're living in an apartment or flat, you can put rose quartz on your balcony or window box, or in potted houseplants.

Angelite helps you understand your pets.

There are different crystals you can put around your home, and you can have fun doing this with your family. You can put them in the hall, kitchen, TV room, bathroom, bedrooms, and anywhere else you can think of.

Selenite and rose quartz also come in heart shapes—this is orange selenite—and these can be lovely to have in different places with their calming energy.

Crystals for your home

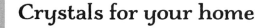

Selenite—helps to cleanse energy in your home

Tourmaline—protects your home from other people's negative energy

Rose quartz—brings loving energy into your home

Amethyst—calms everyone and helps them think about why they feel upset

Titanium quartz—brings in new energy to refresh how your home feels

Calcite (all colors)—comforts and relaxes everyone in your home

Having fun at a crystal party

Ask your parents if you can have a crystal party. Tell them how much fun it will be to laugh and feel happy and enjoy the crystal energy and lovely, sparkly, glowing light. You can have an online party or invite your friends to your home.

Laugh with orange calcite

One of the crystals you can have at your party is orange calcite. This crystal can make you laugh. Sit and hold your orange calcite crystal and imagine a laugh in your tummy moving up very slowly to your chest, and then very, very slowly into your face, and then let the laugh come out through your mouth.

Crystal games

For each game you will need lots of small tumble-polished stones (see page 17).

Recognize different crystals

Take a few crystals out of your collection and show them to your friends. Ask them if they know which crystal is which. If they're not sure, they can look them up in the Crystal Finder (see page 76). Then they can show you their crystals and you can try to name theirs.

Crystal stories

Look at one of your crystals and see what character or animal shape it has. Maybe it looks like a dinosaur or a bear, or maybe it has the face of a princess or an old man. Then make up a story about that character or animal shape. You can use the rest of your crystals to make pictures connected to your story by arranging them on a table or on the floor. You and your friends could each take one bit of the story and make a picture for it with the crystals you have.

Sometimes crystals are carved into the shapes of animals, like this rabbit.

Crystal songs

Why not try making up a song or a poem about crystals? Here's one to get you started:

**Jasper is red, lapis is blue,
Here is a rose quartz that's pink and
for you!**

Crystal art

Make a picture of your favorite crystal by using pastels, paints, or coloring pencils. You can also make a mood board in the color of your crystal. For example, jade is green, so you could look in magazines or outside in nature and find the color of jade from a leaf on a tree or a flower, or even a green chocolate wrapper or a green picture. Once you've made your mood board, you can put it on your wall to remind you of your crystal.

Lovely thoughts game

With you and your friends sitting in a circle, you hold a rose quartz crystal and say all the good things you like about everyone else in the circle. Then you pass the crystal filled with your lovely thoughts to the person on your right, who says their nice things about everyone in the circle, before they pass the crystal to the person next to them. Do this until the crystal comes back to you. (If everyone has a rose quartz crystal, there's no need to pass a crystal round the circle—everyone can hold their own crystal and take turns in the same way to say all the good things they like about each other.)

Swopsy!

Give your friends crystals that will be good for them. Swop one of your crystals that you think will be better for them with one of theirs that they think will be good for you. You can also tell each other why you think the crystal you have chosen for them will help them. If you're not sure which crystals to swop, try asking your pendulum (see pages 36–37).

Make a picture of your favorite crystal by using pastels, paints, or coloring pencils

STEP BY STEP · MEDITATION

A MAGICAL JOURNEY WITH YOUR FRIENDS

This meditation is lovely to do with one or more of your friends in person or online, working with a crystal of friendship (see box below). Ask your pendulum or listen to your intuition to help you choose which one. You and your friends can take turns to choose a crystal for all of you for each time you do the meditation.

1 Find a comfortable place to sit with your friend or friends and hold the crystal you or your friend has chosen.

2 You and your friends all close your eyes and take a slow, deep breath in through your noses as you count to 4 in your heads, then breathe out slowly through your mouths as you count to 5 in your heads. Repeat this three times, then breathe normally. Wait a moment before carrying on to make sure everyone is ready.

3 Open your eyes, then read out the meditation on the next page to your friends while they keep their eyes closed.

Crystals of friendship

Sodalite

Rose quartz

Falcon's eye

Citrine

Dalmatian stone

"Imagine we are in a boat going down a magical red river. When we look in the water, the pebbles are all red jasper and we're happy to be together and having fun.

As the boat is traveling along, we notice the river starts to turn orange and the plants by the side of the river have orange flowers and the stones are all orange like carnelian.

The river then goes round a bend and there are beautiful golden yellow trees and birds singing. The river turns golden yellow like citrine, with a shiny light all around us. It feels like we're in our very own Disney World.

In front of us is a sparkling green cave that looks like aventurin,e and as our boat starts to go inside, the river turns green and all the stones in this magical sparkly cave are green, too.

As we travel further into the cave, everything begins to turn into a wonderful pale blue, like blue lace agate, and it's like the sky all around us on a summer's day.

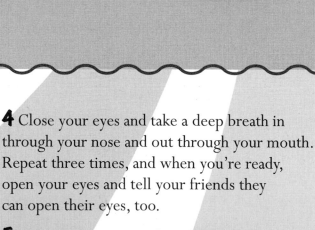

4 Close your eyes and take a deep breath in through your nose and out through your mouth. Repeat three times, and when you're ready, open your eyes and tell your friends they can open their eyes, too.

5 Talk about the magical experience with your friends and how it made you all feel.

We are loving this amazing, magical, mystical journey as we notice how the pale blue sparkly walls of the cave and the river suddenly become darker blue, like the night sky with stars glittering all around us. It looks like lapis lazuli.

Suddenly we see a very bright glowing purple light, and we realize we are on a lake in a massive amethyst cave and it's full of light and dark purple sparkly crystals everywhere.

As our boat starts to float out of the cave, even though our crystal journey is coming to an end, it's only the beginning of exciting new adventures we can go on together with our crystals."

CHAPTER 5

Your crystal finder

This chapter will help you identify any crystals you already have, and choose the crystals you want to work with yourself and to help your friends and family.

Using the crystal finder

Here are over 101 crystals arranged in color groups that can help you feel better and heal you from different things you may need help with.

Finding crystals

If you know a crystal's name, you can look it up in the index (see page 127) to find it and see what it does. If you don't know its name, you can look in the color section and find the crystal from its picture. So, if you have a green crystal and you don't know what it's called, just look through the green section to find it and discover how amazing it is and what it can do for you.

Descriptions

Each crystal has a description of what it looks like and where it comes from. Some crystals, like quartz and amethyst, are found in lots of places all over the world, while others are only found in one or two places, like blue lace agate from Namibia and tiger's eye from South Africa. We'll tell you the different countries where the crystals we talk about in this book come from.

Sometimes special words that you might not have heard before are used to describe crystals, so we have put these words in bold and explained them for you.

Chakras

The chakras (see page 33) that are linked to each crystal are listed so you can see where to put them on yourself or your friends (see pages 64–65). Whenever it says "all chakras," it means that crystal can be put on any of the seven chakras.

How it helps

"How it helps" explains all the special healing things that the crystal you're reading about can do. This can help you decide if it's the crystal you want or need right now.

If you're unwell

If you're feeling unwell, such as you have a very painful tummy ache, are sick, or have a fever, it's important for you to tell an adult and to go with them to the doctor if they say so. The doctor can give you medicine to make you better. Crystals will help you by being there to comfort you and are really good to have with you when you have medicine, as they can help you feel calm and relaxed and get better quicker.

SPECIAL CRYSTALS

This section gives three of the most popular and powerful crystals, which are quartz, amethyst, and rose quartz.

Quartz

There are many types of quartz. Over 70% of the Earth's surface is made of quartz in different ways, such as crystals, rocks, and pebbles you can find on a beach. Amethyst is violet-colored quartz and rose quartz is pink. Both get their color from the minerals (see page 10) inside them, iron and manganese.

Quartz is called "the healing crystal" because it helps with almost anything. If you don't know what to do to help a friend, give them a quartz crystal.

Quartz has been loved by us for thousands of years. Both healers and scientists work with quartz. From healing sickness to making you feel better when you're sad or worried, and from simple science in school to quantum physics and spaceships, crystals are part of the oldest stories and our own modern world. Crystals is the place science and magic meet!

Many types of quartz are covered in this chapter. This section is about beautiful quartz crystal.

Quartz crystal

● ● ● ● ● ● ● **CHAKRA:** all chakras

These are hexagonal crystals (see page 16). They are clear or white and sometimes they have other little crystals inside them (like tourmalinated quartz—see page 103). They are found all over the world, but ones in shops are usually from Arkansas in the USA, Brazil, China, Madagascar, Russia, the Republic of South Africa, or Tibet. Some people call them clear quartz or rock crystal.

HOW IT HELPS: Quartz crystal can help you with almost anything. It also helps you focus when you meditate (see page 49). It can lift you up if you're feeling down, and make you feel better.

Quartz is really good at taking away pain in your body, like a headache or tummy ache. It helps backache, ears, hearing, and balance (like when you get dizzy and may fall over). It's also good if you're feeling tired.

Amethyst

● **CHAKRA:** crown

This is a type of quartz which is violet-colored because it has manganese and iron (which are types of mineral—see page 10) inside it. It is found all over the world, especially in Brazil, India, Madagascar, the Republic of South Africa, and Uruguay.

HOW IT HELPS: This helps to calm you when you're nervous, and makes you feel better when you're anxious and worrying. It's a brilliant crystal to help you meditate (see page 49): hold two small amethyst tumble-polished stones, one in each hand, when you meditate, and you will find it easier to focus your mind. It's good for letting emotions out like anger and being scared. Amethyst helps you sleep—it keeps nightmares away and brings you good dreams, so you remember them in the morning. It also helps you get through upsetting times, like if you lose a pet or friend or someone in your family. It stops you being lonely, like when you're away from home and you have homesickness, and can stop you getting upset if someone says something about you that you don't like. It can help you make your aura big and strong (see page 31). Amethyst is a good crystal to help you make choices when you have changes going on, like moving schools or going to a new club after school. Amethyst makes you feel good about yourself, so it helps if you have to stand up in front of people and speak.

It helps acne, cold and flu, headaches, hearing, and migraines, and your bones, tummy, skin, and teeth. Amethyst crystal washing water (see page 48) is good for your joints if they get hurt, like if you fall over and hurt your knee or twist your ankle in the playground.

Amethyst can help other crystals work better too!

Rose quartz

● **CHAKRA:** heart

This is a pink **crystalline** rock. A crystalline rock is a rock made of millions of really tiny crystals which are so small that you can't see them one at a time. Rose quartz is found in Brazil, India, Madagascar, and the Republic of South Africa.

HOW IT HELPS: Rose quartz is the stone of love and friendship. It makes a perfect gift for everyone. It's a very calming crystal, so it helps if you feel upset, angry, sad, anxious, worried, or afraid—so it's a good crystal to have with you if you are scared of things, like spiders, thunder, or heights. It gives you lots of love and helps you forgive anyone who upsets you. It also helps others forgive you if you upset them. Rose quartz changes feelings like jealousy and fear into happiness and being confident in yourself. It opens your imagination, so it helps you be more creative with art, music, and writing.

It helps with aches and pains, coughs, flu, and sunburn.

MULTICOLORED

Multicolored crystals bring lots of good, fun things. These are crystals that you might find in lots of different colors, but all the crystals in a particular group can do certain special things.

Chalcedony

CHAKRA: depends on the type and color

This is a rock which is a type of quartz with other minerals (see page 10) inside it, which make the rock different colors, including blue (see page 97), purple (see page 101), white, pink, black, red, and many more. Some colors of chalcedony have their own names: agate (see page 83) is patterned, carnelian (see page 86) is orange, chrysoprase (see page 92) is green/yellow, flint (see page 107) is gray, jasper (see page 82) comes in many colors, onyx (see page 106) is black, and petrified wood (see page 109) is brown. Chalcedonies are found all around the world.

HOW IT HELPS: These crystals are good if you worry about things that may have happened in the past. They help calm you if you are feeling upset or angry.

Moonstone

● **CHAKRA:** sacral

Moonstones are a type of rock with an amazing shimmering light effect called **chatoyancy**. This is what happens when light goes just a little way into a crystal, bounces around, and then comes out, which makes the crystal look shimmery. Moonstones can be lots of different colors, including white (see page 102), cream, yellow, brown, blue, green, and even a rainbow mixture of colors, too (see page 110). Moonstones come from India.

HOW IT HELPS: These are very calming stones and help you if you're feeling angry about someone who has upset you—the crystals gently soothe you, so you can forgive the person who hurt your feelings. They are good if you worry what other children say about you. Although moonstones don't come from the moon, they can help you feel the moon's energy when it's bright in the sky at night. This can help you try something new if you always do the same things and want a change, and can also help you make new friends. Moonstones look after you when you travel, like on a vacation, keeping you happy and safe on the journey. They also help make a happy home.

Moonstone crystal washing waters (see page 48) are good for insect bites, and your skin and hair.

Jasper

● **CHAKRA:** base, but specific jaspers may also be linked to other chakras

These are another type of chalcedony (see page 81) in solid colors—they are **opaque**, which means you can't see through them. They can be red (see page 84), yellow (see page 89), green, brown, blue, and purple, and sometimes have mixed colors and patterns, like bloodstone (see page 91), which is green and red. They are found all over the world.

HOW IT HELPS: These are good crystals to have when you're feeling sad—for example, they can help you if you have homesickness and are feeling lonely. Jaspers can also help you focus when you use your pendulum (see pages 36–37).

If you feel a little unwell, like with a cough or a cold, they can help you get better, and they help keep you healthy when you are well, too. They are good for backache and muscle cramps.

Tourmaline

● ● ● ● ● ● ● **CHAKRA:** all chakras, but specific tourmalines may also be particularly linked to some chakras

These crystals come in most colors, including green (see page 92), blue, pink (see page 95), red, yellow, black (see page 105), brown, and lavender, as well as colorless. They may also have two or three colors in the same crystal, such as green or blue with a pink center, or lime green with a white center. They are found around the world, but mostly in Brazil and Pakistan.

HOW IT HELPS: A tourmaline crystal is like a lucky charm that looks after you and keeps you well. It's good if you are sad, lonely, or missing a special friend. It can keep your mind focused when everything around you seems to be changing, like moving to a new school, and can help you meditate (see page 49). Tourmalines boost your confidence and can help if you worry about what others are thinking about you.

They are also good for your tummy.

Fluorite

● **CHAKRA:** brow

These crystals are usually shaped, like cubes and diamond shapes, and can be lots of different colors, including purple (see page 100), clear, blue, green, yellow, brown, pink, red, black, and rainbow-colored (see page 110). They are found worldwide, especially in China, Europe, Mexico, the Republic of South Africa, and the USA.

HOW IT HELPS: These crystals soothe you if you are feeling worried or anxious. They help you make decisions, like if you want pizza or pasta or if you want to wear red or blue today. They help you to stay in touch with friends if you're away from each other, whether you're in your own homes or a long way away from each other, like friends you meet on holiday and want to stay friends with. They make meditation easy by helping you focus your mind.

Fluorites also stop your eyes aching if you spend too much time on your computer, phone, or games console. They are good for your bones and teeth, as well as backache, colds, and flu.

Agate

CHAKRA: depends on the type and color

These are a type of chalcedony (see page 81) which have bands or patterns and come in many colors, including blue (see page 96), black (see page 104), brown (see page 109), gray (see page 107), pink (see page 93), and many more. Agates are found worldwide.

HOW IT HELPS: These crystals make you feel safe and give you strength if you feel worried or anxious. They boost your natural skills, making you even better at the things you already do well. Agate also helps you meditate (see page 49).

They can help an upset tummy and are good for your eyesight.

Calcite

● ● ● ● ● ● ●
CHAKRA: all chakras, but specific calcites may also be particularly linked to some chakras

These are found worldwide as rocks and crystals in lots of colors, including green (see page 90), blue (see page 97), yellow, gold (see page 88), orange (see page 86), clear, white, brown, pink, red (see page 85), black, and gray.

HOW IT HELPS: Calcites help soothe you if you get worried, anxious, or panicky, and they make you feel better. They can calm you down if you are overexcited. A calcite is a good crystal to have at school, as it can help you learn things, like art, numbers, reading, and writing.

RED

Red crystals make you feel strong inside if you are feeling upset or worried.

Red jasper

● **CHAKRA:** base

This jasper (see page 82) is found as a rock in Brazil and India.

HOW IT HELPS: It helps you remember your dreams and enjoy what you are doing while you are doing it. It can give you new ideas so you can work out what you want to do next, such as starting a new creative project at school or decorating your bedroom with posters and things you like. It's good for meditation (see page 49), because it helps you feel grounded (see opposite) and think about what is happening right now, not about things that have happened or will happen.

Red jasper can help stop you from getting unwell, and it keeps you safe.

Garnet

● **CHAKRA:** base

This is found as small crystals in China, Russia, the Republic of South Africa, and the USA.

HOW IT HELPS: Garnet makes you feel better by helping you control your emotions, such as if something is upsetting you or you are feeling angry. It gives you creative energy to finish things you need to do—like your schoolwork or keeping your room tidy—and it gives you a boost of energy when you're feeling tired, especially if you have lots of homework to do or are playing sports, like football or swimming.

Harlequin quartz

● **CHAKRA:** base

This is found as a quartz crystal with other crystals growing inside it (see page 79). It is found worldwide, especially in China and Madagascar.

HOW IT HELPS: Harlequin quartz helps you concentrate and makes it easier for you to say how you feel, so it's good if you have ADHD. It can relieve anxiety and panic attacks and is good for grounding (see opposite). It makes it easier to find friends and talk to new people. You can put larger harlequin quartz crystals in your room to make a beautiful, loving, and calming space.

This crystal gives you physical energy when you're feeling tired but you still have things to do, such as homework or an after-school activity. It makes your legs, knees, ankles, feet, and lower back stronger and helps if they are hurt or aching.

Falcon's eye

● **CHAKRA:** base

This is a rock which looks like it's shimmering because of an effect called chatoyancy (see page 81). It comes from the Republic of South Africa, and is sometimes also called red tiger's eye.

HOW IT HELPS: Falcon's eye helps you cope with emotional upsets, such as friendship worries or if you can't sleep at night. When you need to do something you've been afraid to do, it gives you courage. It helps you be practical so you can get things done, like your schoolwork or tidying your room.

It also eases the pain of sunburn.

Red calcite

● **CHAKRA:** base

This calcite crystal (see page 83) is found as a rock in Mexico, with a surface that feels smooth when you touch it.

HOW IT HELPS: This crystal can help you feel grounded (see right). It reassures you if you have a panic attack or feel anxious, and is great for helping you if you are stuck in a pattern of behavior (like OCD). Red calcite is also a powerful stone that can help you focus (for example, if you have ADHD).

Strawberry aventurine

● **CHAKRA:** base

This is a type of quartz with little bits of hematite or goethite inside, making it sparkly. This rock is found in Brazil, Canada, China, India, Italy, Madagascar, Nepal, the Republic of South Africa, Russia, and Turkey, and is sometimes called red aventurine.

HOW IT HELPS: This crystal is kind to you if you feel sad or low, and gets you going again. If you are finding things difficult, it gives you more confidence and makes you feel strong from the inside out, and it is also grounding (see below). It brings excitement to things you're doing that you wouldn't expect to be exciting! It helps you laugh at yourself when you do something funny. If you're having arguments or upsets with your parents or your brothers or sisters, try putting small strawberry aventurine stones around your house to help make things better. (Check with an adult that this is okay.)

Strawberry aventurine is good if you get hurt, such as if you fall over in the playground and graze your knee, because it helps your body to heal. It gives you a burst of energy and is good for your blood and the way it moves inside you. Strawberry aventurine crystal washing water (see page 48) is good for keeping your skin healthy and well.

Grounding crystals

We say that some crystals can help you feel "grounded." This means that when you're working with a grounding crystal's energy, such as by holding it or looking at it, it feels as though your feet are growing roots like a tree that go deep into the ground, and it gives you a calm energy from the inside out.

ORANGE

Orange crystals bring you happiness.

Orange calcite

● **CHAKRA:** sacral

This calcite crystal (see page 83) is found as a rock which has a waxy feel when you touch it. It comes from Mexico.

HOW IT HELPS: This crystal helps you laugh, have fun, and feel happy, because it brings happy energy. It picks you up if you're feeling sad. It can also be soothing and calming, especially if you are feeling angry! It makes you more confident and can also give you ideas if you're feeling stuck.

Sunstone

● **CHAKRA:** crown

This crystal is very sparkly and bright because of the different minerals (see page 10) inside it, including hematite (see page 106). It comes from India.

HOW IT HELPS: Sunstone does what it says! When you hold it, it feels like the sun is shining on you. It can chase away the feeling of being frightened and scared, and helps if you are feeling worried. It boosts energy and helps you feel strong when you need to.

Sunstone also helps if you have a sore throat, if you hurt your knee, elbow, wrist, or ankle, or if you have backache or aching feet.

Carnelian

● **CHAKRA:** sacral

This is a type of chalcedony (see page 81) that forms orange pebbles and is found all over the world. The ones you find in shops usually come from Brazil, India, and Uruguay.

HOW IT HELPS: Carnelian is a "feel better stone." It helps you feel good about yourself! It's great for giving you energy when you're tired and need a little boost, especially on days when you're feeling a little lazy. Carnelian can give you courage if you're finding things difficult or are afraid to say what you want, so it's really helpful for dealing with your emotions if you feel angry, jealous, or sad. It can help you remember things and focus on your schoolwork or anything else, like games or sports.

Carnelian helps you get your appetite back if you're off your food, and is good for digestion and helping your food go down. This crystal can help you feel better if you have a cold. It can also help if you have any pain like a tummy ache.

Tangerine quartz

● ● ● CHAKRA: base, sacral, and solar plexus

This quartz crystal is found mostly in Brazil and Madagascar, and is an orange to red-orange color because of hematite (see page 106) on the outside of it.

HOW IT HELPS: Tangerine quartz helps you make friends easily and forgive people who have upset you. It makes you feel calm and helps you stop worrying. It gives you confidence and helps you have fun and laugh with your friends.

Tangerine quartz is good for your tummy, so it makes any tummy aches better and can help if you are overweight. This crystal can also give you extra energy.

Peach aventurine

● CHAKRA: sacral

This is a type of quartz with little bits of pyrite (see page 107) and mica inside it, which makes it sparkly. It comes from India.

HOW IT HELPS: Peach aventurine gives you positivity and confidence, which can bring you good luck. It also makes you less shy. It's a really good crystal to have when you start to learn how to meditate (see page 49), because it clears worries from your mind and helps you focus and make choices. It also helps you get to sleep at night.

This crystal is good for helping your muscles become strong. It also helps with tummy aches, headaches, migraines, and spots.

Orange selenite

● ● CHAKRA: sacral and crown

This crystal is found around the world but mostly in Morocco, the UK, and the USA. Its color is orange to pale peach and it has a **cat's eye** effect. This is similar to chatoyancy (see page 81), but here the light looks like a narrow line on the crystal, which is what cats' eyes look like when light is shone on them. It should not be put into water (see page 41).

HOW IT HELPS: Orange selenite helps you start something new! It can also bring positive change to anything you want to do. It's good for learning spellings or studying for tests because it helps you remember things. It can give you the confidence to stop being friends with people who aren't good for you. It can also calm you down if you're feeling angry.

Orange selenite can help when you have sick feelings in your tummy or when joints, like your ankles or knees, hurt.

YELLOW

Yellow crystals help you to be creative.

Golden calcite

● **CHAKRA:** solar plexus

This calcite crystal (see page 83) comes from China, and each crystal looks like a squashed golden rectangle.

HOW IT HELPS: Golden calcite brings lots of positivity to everything you do! This crystal calms you if you feel anxious and makes you feel safe and secure. It gives you confidence, and lets you speak calmly when you're trying to explain something.

Citrine

● **CHAKRA:** solar plexus

This is a golden-yellow type of quartz which is found in Brazil, China, the Democratic Republic of Congo, Madagascar, and Tibet. The color is caused by heat from volcanoes and from deep underground.

HOW IT HELPS: Citrine is a happy stone and gives you confidence to do all the things you want to do, such as making new friends. It is easier to make choices and decisions to do things with citrine. You can also get rid of anger and fear by letting these feelings go through a citrine crystal, which will change them into positive feelings—simply hold the crystal, use SBIS (see page 53), and feel your anger and fear disappear. Citrine can help you focus on learning your schoolwork and writing stories. It is also known as "the money stone," because as well as wealth, it brings lots of good things, such as health, happiness, and friends.

Citrine is good for your tummy, so can help if you feel sick. It also gives you lots of energy to help you grow, and this energy helps your body get better when you're hurt or not well.

Yellow quartz

● ● **CHAKRA:** solar plexus and brow

These are yellow crystals that are **opaque**, which means you can't see through them. They are found in the Republic of South Africa.

HOW IT HELPS: This crystal helps you keep calm when there's lots going on around you and your mind is busy and you're thinking about lots of things at once. It's calming and helps if you're panicking and worried about something. It's good for confidence, focusing your mind on meditation, and learning from things that have happened to you. Yellow quartz is like a ray of sunshine and brings fun into your life.

Yellow quartz also helps your tummy if you have any food allergies, and gives you a boost of energy when you're feeling tired.

Tiger's eye

● CHAKRA: solar plexus

This is gold in color and found in the Republic of South Africa. The shimmering light effect you see in this stone is called chatoyancy (see page 81).

HOW IT HELPS: It makes you as brave as a tiger and gives you confidence if you're feeling shy. It can help get rid of worry, fear, and bad thoughts. Tiger's eye also makes you feel strong if someone is being horrible to you. It helps your intuition (see page 35). It's a stone that makes you feel good! Tiger's eye can help you focus on schoolwork, projects, and games, and gives you ideas for what you want to do when you grow up.

Tiger's eye is good for your tummy and eyes. If you're unwell or have broken any bones, it helps your body mend itself.

Lucky stone

Lots of people call tiger's eye their lucky stone and like to keep it with them.

Golden healer quartz

● ● ● ● ● ● ●

CHAKRA: all chakras, especially heart

These are quartz crystals that have a yellow coloring on them or inside the crystal. They are found worldwide.

HOW IT HELPS: This crystal calms emotions that upset you, like if you're afraid or worried about something. It makes you feel good about yourself if you've been feeling sad.

This crystal helps to keep you well, and helps you get better if you hurt yourself playing games. It's good for everything, including cuts, bruises, and sunburn.

Amber

● CHAKRA: solar plexus

This is a special mineral (see page 10) that comes from prehistoric trees as old as the dinosaurs. It's yellow, orange, or brown, and found in countries that are next to the Baltic Sea, like Poland, Lithuania, and Latvia, as well as other places around the world.

HOW IT HELPS: Amber is a good luck stone and helps your dreams come true.

An amber crystal washing water (see page 48) helps skin conditions, like eczema. It eases allergies like hay fever, and is calming and soothing. If you hurt yourself, hold it on any cuts and bruises to help them heal quicker.

Yellow jasper

● CHAKRA: solar plexus

This jasper (see page 82) is a yellow type of chalcedony (see page 81) found in the Republic of South Africa.

HOW IT HELPS: This crystal is good because it protects you when you're traveling, and helps if you get a funny tummy on vacation. It also gives you energy.

GREEN

Green crystals can help you get better when you're not feeling well.

Green calcite

● **CHAKRA:** heart

This green calcite rock (see page 83) from Mexico feels waxy, like a candle.

HOW IT HELPS: This is a calming crystal that really helps if you're anxious, and if you get very upset, worry, and have panic attacks.

Amazonite

● **CHAKRA:** heart

This stone is green to blue-green and comes from Brazil, Russia, and the USA.

HOW IT HELPS: It soothes and calms you when you're anxious or nervous, so it's really helpful when you have tests at school. It makes your aura strong (see page 31). When you worry, amazonite can make you feel better. It also helps you to be creative.

Jade

● **CHAKRA:** heart

Jade is usually green, but it's also found in lots of other colors. It comes from Canada, China, Myanmar, South America and the USA.

HOW IT HELPS: It's nice to have jade for your first stone, because people say it makes you happy. Jade can pick you up if you're feeling sad, giving you confidence and courage. If you sometimes bump into things or drop things by mistake, this crystal can help you stop doing that. Put jade under your pillow to have good dreams.

Tree agate

● **CHAKRA:** heart

This is a type of agate (see page 83) from India with green and white patterns that look like plants.

HOW IT HELPS: Plants really like this crystal, so it helps all plants grow, whether inside in pots or outside in nature or your garden or yard. It can also help you be a good gardener and look after your plants. It will help you see the beauty in everything around you. Tree agate is a very calming stone and makes you feel better if you're anxious.

It's good for your bones, eyes, and joints, like knees and wrists. Make jade crystal washing water (see page 48) to help with skin problems like eczema, and you can wash your hair with it if you have any hair problems, too.

Green aventurine

● **CHAKRA:** heart

This is a green quartz from Brazil and India with shiny bits of another crystal called mica inside it, which makes it sparkle in the sun. It comes in other colors, too.

HOW IT HELPS: Aventurine calms and soothes you when you feel sad, or are worried or anxious about something like a test at school. It helps you relax. It's good for creativity, and helps you do the best you can in everything you do. It makes choices easier when you can't make up your mind. Aventurine can help you be a good leader.

Aventurine is good for muscles, so you can become stronger, and it can make your muscles feel better if they hurt. It makes your reactions quicker, which is helpful if you're playing a game where you need to catch a ball.

Chrysocolla

● **CHAKRA:** heart

This stone comes in all sorts of blue and green colors from Peru and the USA.

HOW IT HELPS: This crystal helps if you're feeling sad about something you've done, if you're scared, anxious, or worrying about things (like if you are worried about the environment and how it will affect you when you grow up), or if you lose someone very close to you, like a grandparent, parent, or pet. It helps you get rid of anger. Chrysocolla also brings out your creative side when you want to make something.

Chrysocolla helps if you have a tummy ache, or your muscles and joints, like ankles and knees, hurt.

Bloodstone

● **CHAKRA:** heart

This is a green jasper (see page 82) with red dots and it comes from India.

HOW IT HELPS: Bloodstone is calming, so it's useful if you feel angry or upset. It gives you ideas when you want to make something, like a colorful picture, or write a story, and it takes away any worries you have and gives you courage.

It is also helpful for your joints, like knees and elbows.

Give yourself love

When you love yourself you can feel so much more confident and happier in everything you do. It also helps you believe in yourself more and know you can do anything you want to.

Chrysoprase

● **CHAKRA:** heart

This is a green or lemon chalcedony (see page 81) from Australia.

HOW IT HELPS: Chrysoprase makes you feel better if you are confused, anxious, worried, or scared. It can help you feel confident, especially if you feel everyone is always better than you. Chrysoprase can also help with meditation (see page 49) if you get distracted easily and find it hard to focus. It helps you be more creative and skillful when using your hands to make things.

Green tourmaline

● ● **CHAKRA:** heart and brow

This is a green tourmaline crystal (see page 82) with lines running up and down its sides called **striations**. It comes from Brazil and Pakistan.

HOW IT HELPS: This crystal helps you to see your own good ideas, thoughts, and feelings, so it is really good at stopping you from worrying, and makes it easier for you to help other children when they are feeling sad or lonely. It helps you with creative things like making pictures.

Green tourmaline is good for your eyes and helps to keep you well.

Peridot

● **CHAKRA:** heart

This is found as small green crystals and comes from Afghanistan, Brazil, the Canary Islands, Pakistan, Russia, Sri Lanka, and the USA.

HOW IT HELPS: If you're feeling sad or anxious, or you have feelings trapped inside you that you can't explain, peridot can help you feel happy again. It's good for getting rid of anger and jealousy, and wards off laziness. This crystal helps you to focus your thoughts when you meditate (see page 49).

Peridot is good for your tummy, especially if you feel a bit sick after eating. It can help keep you healthy and put on any weight that you've lost when you've been unwell. It can help if you have problems with your eyes or sunburn.

PINK

Pink crystals give you love.

Pink banded agate

● ● **CHAKRA:** sacral and heart

This agate stone (see page 83) has pink and white patterns and comes from Botswana.

HOW IT HELPS: It brings out your creative side—for example, if you're drawing and painting lovely pictures or making pretty jewelry or model airplanes or cars. If you feel sad, holding this happy stone can help you feel better.

Kunzite

● **CHAKRA:** heart

A crystal with lines running up and down its sides called **striations**, which comes from Afghanistan.

HOW IT HELPS: This crystal helps you to keep calm when you get overexcited and if you're worrying about anything. It makes you feel confident about yourself, so everything is nicer for you, like making new friends and talking to other children and adults. Kunzite helps you meditate (see page 49).

Morganite

● **CHAKRA:** heart

A pink type of crystal with pink lines on it, called **striations**, going up the crystal. It comes from Brazil and Pakistan.

HOW IT HELPS: Morganite fills you up with love. It helps you keep calm and stops you arguing with your friends and family. It's good for meditation (see page 49), because it clears your mind. Sometimes when you meditate holding morganite, you can see new ways of doing things better.

It's also good for chest conditions like coughs, and helps all healing if you're hurt or unwell.

Striations

Striations are natural lines running up the sides of a crystal that are formed as the crystal grows.

Strawberry quartz

● ● **CHAKRA:** heart and crown

This strawberry pink crystal looks just like mashed-up strawberries! It comes from the Republic of South Africa.

HOW IT HELPS: This crystal calms and soothes you, so it helps if you can't sleep, and it gives you love, meaning you can love yourself.

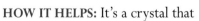

Rhodochrosite

● **CHAKRA:** heart

This is found as a pink bumpy stone or a small crystal, and comes from Argentina. When it is polished, it has pretty pink and cream patterns.

HOW IT HELPS: It's a crystal that makes good things happen and brings you fun things and happiness. It gives you enthusiasm, such as making it more exciting for you if you play a musical instrument or want to learn. It gives you courage and helps you if you're feeling sad or anxious. It is also good for your memory.

Rhodonite

● **CHAKRA:** heart

This crystal can be found as either pink rocks or red crystals in Australia, Cornwall in the UK, Madagascar, the Republic of South Africa, and the USA.

HOW IT HELPS: This crystal is really good if you like music or playing musical instruments, because it makes you feel confident so you can play the best you can. It also calms anxiety and can help you focus your mind. If you feel upset about things like your parents telling you off or having an argument with a friend, then this crystal will help you feel better. And rhodonite is good for everyone's memory, so is helpful for tests at school.

It's good for your bones, eyes that hurt in bright light, and throat infections.

Pink tourmaline

● **CHAKRA:** heart

This is a pink type of tourmaline (see page 82) with lines running up and down its sides, which are called **striations**. It comes from Brazil.

HOW IT HELPS: This crystal gives you courage and confidence for doing new things, like starting a new school, going to a new club, or making friends. It can help you come up with new ideas and makes it easier to share the things you love, like your favorite crystals. It can also make you feel better if you are hurt by something a friend says or does.

Pink tourmaline crystal washing water (see page 48) is good for your skin, keeping it healthy and helping it heal if you have skin problems.

Rubellite

● ● **CHAKRA:** base and heart

This is a dark pink tourmaline crystal (see page 82) from Brazil.

HOW IT HELPS: It helps you if you find it hard to say things in a kind way.

It's good for your tummy, and gives you lots of energy.

Pink opal

● **CHAKRA:** heart

This is a pale pink color and comes from Peru.

HOW IT HELPS: This crystal helps to calm your mind when you are feeling confused. It reminds you that you are loved. If you find it hard to keep your mind focused, it helps you meditate (see page 49).

Pink opal is good for your lungs and heart, and helps diabetes. You can also soothe itchy skin by washing it with pink opal crystal washing water (see page 48).

Crystal names

Some crystals are named after what they look like— strawberry quartz looks like mashed-up strawberries! Others are named after their color, and sometimes that's in another language: *rhodo* means rosy in Greek, so we have rhodonite and rhodochrosite.

BLUE

Blue crystals are calming and help you say how you are feeling.

Aquamarine

● **CHAKRA:** throat

This is a blue/green crystal that is found in Afghanistan, Brazil, Namibia, Pakistan, and the USA.

HOW IT HELPS: Whether you're going to school or far away on vacation, aquamarine keeps you safe while you're traveling. It's a calming crystal that helps you if you get angry or upset because of something someone says or does, and it also gives you courage to say what you need to. It's a good crystal to help you stay focused, which is great for learning new things at school and meditating (see page 49).

Aquamarine is good for your eyes and teeth, as well as swollen joints (like knees and ankles) and swollen glands. It's also good for any kind of travel sickness (air, sea, car, or train).

Blue lace agate

● **CHAKRA:** throat

This agate stone (see page 83) has bands of pale blue and white and is found in Namibia.

HOW IT HELPS: This is a very gentle and soothing stone which helps you if you are feeling worried or anxious. It keeps you calm, so you can express yourself and tell your friends or parents how you are feeling. It's good for speech, so can help if you have a stammer or find it hard to say some words when you're upset.

It can help you heal if you break or fracture a bone, and is good for your eyesight. Blue lace agate crystal washing water (see page 48) is good for your nails and hair.

Nodules

Crystals that are nodules are knobbly because they tend to grow in something else. Imagine a rock growing in thick mud. The rock is harder than the mud, so will keep growing, but some bits of the mud will be thicker than others and alter how easy it is for the rock to grow, so the rock grows with bumps instead of a smooth surface.

Celestite

● **CHAKRA:** brow

This is a beautiful pale blue crystal from Madagascar. It should not be put into water (see page 41).

HOW IT HELPS: This crystal brings out your creativity when you're making things, painting, and writing stories. It can also help you say what you feel and find the right words to say. It's really good to help you relax if you're feeling anxious or worried. It helps you remember your dreams and keeps nightmares away so you can sleep well. Celestite helps you get better at things you love doing and are naturally good at—for example, art, music, or sport. It helps you spread love to all your friends. When you meditate (see page 49) with celestite, it can take you into beautiful places in your imagination. You feel like you're in a magical place surrounded by angels and fairies. It's like a lovely dream that you can be creative with. Celestite can also give you calming, peaceful feelings when you meditate with it.

It's good for your eyes and ears, and helps stop pain.

Blue calcite

● **CHAKRA:** throat

This calcite crystal (see page 83) is a blue rock that feels like wax. It comes from Mexico.

HOW IT HELPS: This is a very calming crystal. It keeps nightmares and bad dreams away, and helps you sleep at night and remember your good dreams.

Blue calcite is good for your throat and tonsils.

Blue chalcedony

● **CHAKRA:** throat

This type of chalcedony (see page 81) is a pale blue stone from the Republic of South Africa.

HOW IT HELPS: It helps you say how you are feeling to your friends and parents, and it can help your parents and teachers understand how you're feeling, too.

Angelite

● **CHAKRA:** throat

These are blue and white **nodules**, which means they have a bumpy, knobbly surface, and they come from Peru.

HOW IT HELPS: This crystal makes you feel confident and helps you ask your guardian angel for help when you need it. It can also help you talk and listen to your pets and animal friends. It helps you not to be angry or jealous about things other children have, and to feel happy for them to have nice things. If you have a bath in angelite crystal washing water (see page 48), it can cleanse your energy, just like when you cleanse your crystals (see page 40).

It's also good for your throat and senses (seeing, hearing, smelling, tasting, and touching).

Aqua aura

● ● **CHAKRA:** throat and brow

This is an amazing, beautiful, bright blue and mostly clear quartz crystal mixed with gold. We call gold a precious mineral (see page 10) because it can be hard to find. This crystal comes from the USA.

HOW IT HELPS: This crystal makes your aura strong (see page 31). This protects you, as if you have a shield of armor or a bubble around you, and bounces away energy that you don't like. It can help you be happy again if you're feeling sad. It helps if you've lost someone you love, like a grandparent, parent, or even a pet, and makes you feel better.

Lapis lazuli

● **CHAKRA:** brow

This is a blue rock made up of three crystals: lazurite, calcite (see page 83), and pyrite (see page 107). It comes from Afghanistan and Chile.

HOW IT HELPS: It has a calm energy that helps you to relax and say how you feel, so you feel better. It's good for helping you with things you are naturally good at—for example, sports or singing. It helps you sleep well and remember your dreams. It's also a good crystal to help you get organized, such as with your homework and putting things in places that you can find them.

Lapis lazuli is good for your bones, throat, ears, and hearing, as well as backache and keeping you well. It helps if you feel giddy (the feeling you get when you've been spinning round too much!).

Kyanite

● **CHAKRA:** throat

This is a flat crystal from Brazil. It is usually blue but can also be found in other colors, including black, gray, white, green, yellow, and pink.

HOW IT HELPS: Kyanite helps you say what you're feeling and be peaceful and calm. It can help to balance the energy moving through each of your chakras (see page 33). It makes it easier to focus when you start meditating (see page 49). It can also help you to remember your dreams.

This crystal is good for your throat and muscles—it relaxes your throat muscles, meaning it's great for singing!

Sodalite

● **CHAKRA:** brow

This is a blue or blue and white stone and it comes from Brazil.

HOW IT HELPS: This is a calming stone. It's good for groups of friends to share (or you can each have your own) as it connects you all as a team. It helps you express yourself creatively, with things like music, singing, painting, and drawing, and say how you're feeling. It boosts your energy and confidence so helps if you're feeling sensitive, afraid, or worried—for example, if you worry you could be doing better at school or sports. If you're feeling confused, it can help your mind to focus.

Sodalite can help you get to sleep.

Turquoise

● **CHAKRA:** throat

This stone's color ranges from blue to green and it comes from China, Myanmar, Tibet, and the USA.

HOW IT HELPS: This crystal brings good luck to everything you do, so it can help you avoid accidents, like falling over in the playground or dropping things. It gives you the courage to make new friends, speak in front of others, and say how you are feeling, and it can make you feel better if you've been worrying. It can help you enjoy eating if you don't like your food. It's good for sharing love with your friends and family. Turquoise really helps if you're traveling on any journey, like a trip around the world with your family or a walk to the corner store, because it protects travelers and guides you along the way so you don't get lost. It's also good for any travel sickness (air, car, sea, or train). Turquoise takes you on a magical journey when you're meditating (see page 49), like you're traveling to the moon and back, and gives you a lovely feeling of relaxation. It helps you imagine pictures in your mind, which is good for meditating, too, as well as writing stories and doing schoolwork.

It is a good crystal to help you stay well when you are, so that you don't get ill. It's good for your joints, like ankles and elbows, chest (so it can help things like colds and flu), and throat, tummy, and muscles. It helps headache or backache go away and helps heal cuts and grazes. It's also good for allergies like hay fever or when the air is polluted from too many cars and lorries. Turquoise can help your eyes and skin conditions, especially if these get worse when you are upset.

Hawk's eye

● ● **CHAKRA:** throat and brow

This is blue tiger's eye (see page 89) from the Republic of South Africa.

HOW IT HELPS: This helps settle an upset tummy. It's good for your throat and tonsils, and throat infections.

VIOLET

Violet crystals help you to feel calm and peaceful.

Purple fluorite

● **CHAKRA:** crown

This crystal looks like steps. It is deep purple in color but often is white or clear underneath. It comes from Mexico.

HOW IT HELPS: Purple fluorite makes it easier to learn new things. It makes you feel better if your eyes hurt and you are tired after spending a lot of time watching TV or playing computer games.

It's good for your bones, teeth, and gums.

Lepidolite

● ● **CHAKRA:** heart and brow

This crystal is a lavender color. Sometimes it is found as a stone, and sometimes it is made up of layers that look like the side view of the pages of a closed book. It comes from Brazil.

HOW IT HELPS: It helps you with learning and doing schoolwork. It can comfort you if you are feeling worried or anxious and if things are changing around you, like moving home or starting a new school. It can help your garden blossom, so you have lots of flowers, fruit, and vegetables.

It's good for tummy ache (when you've eaten too much) and muscle cramps.

Spirit quartz

● **CHAKRA:** crown

This is amethyst crystals with lots of baby crystals growing off their sides. It can also be clear or white quartz. It comes from the Republic of South Africa.

HOW IT HELPS: It gives a sense of belonging, so it's good for any group of friends or club—for example, it helps sports teams bond and play as a team—and it can help you make new friends. It helps you to feel better about yourself, especially if you feel sad or lonely. If you feel stuck doing the same thing, it encourages you to do something new and different. It makes meditation (see page 49) easier if you find it difficult, and helps you to have nice dreams and remember them in the morning. It's a magical stone that brings you good luck.

Spirit quartz crystal washing water (see page 48) is good for skin allergies.

Banded amethyst

● ● **CHAKRA:** brow and crown

This crystal is purple with white stripes. It comes from Brazil, India, Russia, and Zambia.

HOW IT HELPS: This crystal helps if you keep getting a pain that won't go away. It's also good for headaches and your eyes, tummy, and chest.

Purple chalcedony

● **CHAKRA:** crown

This is a lavender to violet type of chalcedony (see page 81) from the USA.

HOW IT HELPS: This brings out the best in you, helping you to be kind, generous, and caring, such as making time to help a friend. It helps you be part of a group, because it makes you feel like you belong. It helps you forgive anyone who has upset you, like a friend or brother or sister, so you can be friends again.

Charoite

● **CHAKRA:** crown

This is a violet stone which sometimes has white quartz and black manganese inside. It comes from Russia.

HOW IT HELPS: Charoite helps you meditate (see page 49) and be mindful (see page 53).

It's good for all aches and pains, including headaches. It's also good for your eyes.

Sugilite

This is a purple rock found in the Republic of South Africa.

● **CHAKRA:** crown

HOW IT HELPS: This crystal gives you confidence and courage. It helps you to forgive anyone who has upset you, like a friend or brother or sister, so you can be friends again. It also helps you let go of feelings, like anger or jealousy, so they don't tie you in knots.

It's good for children with any learning difficulties, like dyslexia. It eases pain if anything hurts, like a headache or upset tummy.

WHITE AND CLEAR

White and clear crystals help your intuition and give you positive energy.

White moonstone

● **CHAKRA:** sacral

This moonstone (see page 81) is a white rock from India that shows chatoyancy (see page 81).

HOW IT HELPS: White moonstone is really good for new starts, like making new friends, going to a new club, or starting a new school, because it gives you confidence to do positive things and calms you when you feel worried. It helps you be kind to your younger brothers or sisters. It's a happy stone and when you hold it you can smile. It also helps your intuition (see page 35).

It's good for energy and your eyesight, and it soothes insect bites. Washing your skin and hair with white moonstone crystal washing water (see page 48) keeps them well.

Dalmatian stone

● **CHAKRA:** base

This is white with black dots, just like a Dalmatian dog. It is made of white quartz and the dots are patches of black tourmaline (see page 105). It is found in Mexico.

HOW IT HELPS: This crystal can help you at school, because it is calming and makes worries and anxiety go away, creating a space in your mind to focus on your schoolwork. It gives you lots of positive energy so you can be good at games and sports. It can help you make good friends and keep everyone happy.

It's also good for muscle sprains and cramps.

Herkimer diamond

● **CHAKRA:** crown

This is a clear, short, and thick **double-terminated** quartz crystal. Double-terminated means the crystal has points, which are called **terminations**, on each end. It only comes from Herkimer County, New York State, USA. There are other "diamond-style" quartz crystals you can find from Pakistan, Mexico, Romania, and other places, but although they look like Herkimer diamonds, they are not the same.

HOW IT HELPS: This crystal helps if you feel worried or anxious about big things that are changing, like going to a new school or moving home. It can calm you and make you feel happy again. It helps you be mindful (see page 53) throughout the day. It gives you energy and helps you remember things.

Apophyllite

● ● **CHAKRA:** brow and crown

This crystal may be shaped like a cube or pyramid. It is usually white or colorless, but sometimes it's green. It comes from India.

HOW IT HELPS: It's good for your intuition (see page 35) and can help you meditate (see page 49) any time during the day you want to. It helps you remember all the lovely things you have done.

It's also good for your eyesight.

Snow quartz

● **CHAKRA:** crown

This is a crystal rock, which is called **cryptocrystalline**—this means they are made up of millions of tiny quartz crystals, rather than one large crystal. Snow quartz is found worldwide, especially in India and the USA.

HOW IT HELPS: This crystal helps to clear your mind if it's full of thoughts, so it's very good for meditation (see page 49) and studying for tests.

Howlite

● **CHAKRA:** crown

These have white-looking lumps or bumps, and sometimes have gray markings. They are found in the USA. Howlite is often dyed to make it a different color and used to copy expensive stones, such as turquoise and lapis lazuli.

HOW IT HELPS: It helps you stay calm if you're worried about something, and not get angry or be selfish. It makes it easier to speak in front of people, like your class at school, or to tell your parents or friends how you're feeling. Howlite helps you learn and remember things, so it's good if you have a test. If there is something you really want, like being in the school netball or soccer team, it's also really good for helping you make it happen.

Howlite helps to keep you well and take the hurt away if you fall over in the playground or at home, and can help stop you catching colds and flu. It's good for your teeth and bones.

Tourmalinated quartz

● ● ● ● ● ● **CHAKRA:** all chakras

These are quartz crystals with rods of another crystal called tourmaline (see page 82) growing through it. They come from Brazil.

HOW IT HELPS: Tourmalinated quartz is good if you're feeling sad, worried, and anxious, because it helps you think about the things that are upsetting you and calms your worries so that you can be happy again.

Selenite

● **CHAKRA:** crown

This is a clear or white crystal and it comes from Mexico, Morocco, and the USA. It should not be put into water (see page 41).

HOW IT HELPS: This crystal can help cleanse your other crystals of energy they don't need (see page 40). It can also cleanse you and your aura (see page 31).

It's good for skin conditions, like eczema and psoriasis, and sensitive skin, as well as backache.

BLACK

Black crystals help you to keep grounded (see page 85).

Black banded agate

● **CHAKRA:** base

This is a type of agate (see page 83) which has black and white bands or stripes and comes from India.

HOW IT HELPS: This crystal helps you feel strong from the inside out, so that you feel better and not so upset about changes, like moving home or starting a new school. It can also help you if someone you're close to, like a grandparent, dies and you feel sad.

It's good for your tummy if it's upset when you feel sad, too.

Jet

● **CHAKRA:** base

This crystal comes from trees that lived a long time ago and were turned to stone. It can be found all over the world, especially in Canada, Madagascar, the UK, and the USA.

HOW IT HELPS: It gives both energy and calmness, so it's very soothing if you feel anxious and worried. Jet brings you good luck.

It's also good for an upset tummy, headaches, swollen glands, and colds.

Lodestone

● **CHAKRA:** base

This is the only natural magnet in the world! It's a stone that is black or brown and it feels very heavy for its size. It comes from the USA.

HOW IT HELPS: This crystal is grounding (see page 85). It keeps you mindful (see page 53) all day, gives you confidence, and clears your mind if you're confused. It helps your intuition (see page 35).

It's good for joints, like knees and hips, and aching muscles.

Zebra rock

● **CHAKRA:** sacral

This is a type of quartz with black and white stripes in a "zebra" pattern. It comes from the USA.

HOW IT HELPS: It's good if you like running, as it gives you lots of energy to keep going.

It's good for dry skin and your teeth, gums, bones, and muscles.

Black tourmaline

● **CHAKRA:** base

This is a black tourmaline crystal (see page 82) with lines running up and down its sides, which are called **striations**. It comes from Brazil, India, and Pakistan.

HOW IT HELPS: This crystal helps to protect you from negative energy. It boosts your aura (see page 31) and is good for your intuition (see page 35). It can help you feel better if you're sad, or if you are worried or anxious about something. It gives you ideas and helps you understand things more easily, so is good when you do schoolwork or make things like jewelry or model cars or airplanes. It comforts you if you get upset when you make a mistake. Black tourmaline can help you be more aware of the environment, which means it stops you being clumsy, such as dropping things, falling over, or banging into things, and also means it helps you enjoy nature and notice more of what is going on around you.

It's good for joints, like knees and hips. It can help if you get confused by letters when you're reading (dyslexia).

Snowflake obsidian

● **CHAKRA:** base

This is a type of black obsidian (see below) with white markings that look like snowflakes. It comes from the USA.

HOW IT HELPS: It can calm you if you're feeling angry, and helps if you're feeling lonely or homesick. It can help you focus when you're meditating (see page 49).

Snowflake obsidian is a very special crystal for those children who have upset tummies and runny noses at the same time. It can make both of these better together. It's good for your eyesight and bones, and snowflake obsidian crystal washing water (see page 48) is good for your skin.

Apache tear

● **CHAKRA:** base

This is a small black stone you can see through, and it comes from the USA.

HOW IT HELPS: This crystal helps you when you feel sad, and can help you forgive a friend if they've upset you, so you can be friends again. If you feel a little worried when things change, like if you're going to a new school, it helps you feel better about leaving your old school and old friends, and feel more confident and happier about moving to a new school and class and making new friends.

It's good for your knees, especially if you've hurt them.

Black obsidian

This is a type of glass made by volcanoes in Mexico and the USA.

● **CHAKRA:** base

HOW IT HELPS: This helps you grow up strong. It's grounding (see page 85) and is good for your intuition (see page 35). It's good for creative things, like painting colorful pictures and making things, because it helps you listen to your intuition, which can give you ideas.

It is also good for your tummy.

Shungite

● ● ● ● ● ● ●

CHAKRA: all chakras

This is a black mineral (see page 10) and it comes from Russia.

HOW IT HELPS: In the same way you can cleanse crystals of negative energy (see page 40), this crystal can take away any negative energy you have. It is very calming if you feel worried or anxious.

It's good for getting back to normal after you've been unwell, and helps your body heal if you hurt yourself or have to have surgery in hospital. It's good for allergies.

Black onyx

● **CHAKRA:** base

This is a black type of chalcedony (see page 81) which is found in India and the Republic of South Africa.

HOW IT HELPS: This crystal gives you confidence if you are worried or anxious. It's also grounding (see page 85), so it can help you feel better if you have lost someone close to you, like a grandparent or parent.

It's also good for allergies.

GRAY

Gray crystals give you sparks of energy.

Hematite

● **CHAKRA:** base

This crystal is a shiny, metallic-looking silver-gray color when it's polished (see page 17). Before it's polished, it's a black or red-brown (brick-colored) rock with lots of bumps on its surface, like a bunch of grapes—this is called **botryoidal**. It is found all around the world, but especially in Morocco and the UK.

HOW IT HELPS: Hematite helps if you are worried or anxious, because it gives you courage. It is a grounding crystal (see page 85), so it's good for meditation and mindfulness (see pages 49 and 53). Hematite helps you move your hands and fingers easily where you want them to, so it's great for making things, like model cars or airplanes. It's good if you find math tricky, because it helps your memory and keeps you grounded if your head starts to spin with all the numbers.

This crystal is good for backache, broken bones, and fractures. Hematite crystal washing water (see page 48) helps soothe mild sunburn. Hematite is also good for travel sickness (car, plane, train, or sea), and makes it easier to get to sleep at night.

Flint

● **CHAKRA:** crown

This is a type of chalcedony (see page 81) that is usually gray, but can also be a creamy white or brown. It is a bumpy rock or pebble, and is found all over the world.

HOW IT HELPS: This stone is good for your intuition (see page 35). It helps you understand what people mean when they say something that doesn't make sense. It can help stop nightmares.

It's also good for your tummy, as well as cuts, grazes, and bruises.

Gray banded agate

● **CHAKRA:** sacral

This is a gray and white banded type of agate (see page 83) which comes from Botswana.

HOW IT HELPS: If you get tired or if you're just feeling a little unwell, this crystal can pick you up and help you feel better.

Pyrite

● ● ● ● ● ● ●

CHAKRA: all chakras, but especially solar plexus

This crystal comes in many shapes that often have flat sides, like cubes and pyramids, and is sparkly. It's sometimes called fool's gold, and is found in Peru, Spain, the UK, and the USA.

HOW IT HELPS: Pyrite gives you little boosts of energy that give you creative ideas when you're painting pictures or making models. It's a crystal that can bring you good luck.

This crystal can help stop you snoring. It's good for your tummy and bones.

Flint in the Stone Age

Flint was used to make some of the earliest human tools a long time ago in the Stone Age. These tools included hand axes, arrowheads, scrapers, flakes, and blades.

BROWN

Brown crystals give you confidence and help you enjoy and have a lovely time in nature.

Smoky quartz

● **CHAKRA:** base

This is brown-colored quartz which comes from Brazil, Madagascar, and the USA.

HOW IT HELPS: This crystal is great for sleep, because it helps you have good dreams and keeps nightmares away. It's a magical crystal that can give you energy during the day and relax you at night. It's good if you find it difficult to say how you feel or if you have a stammer, because it keeps your mind clear of distracting thoughts. If you feel angry or sad, smoky quartz is soothing and helps you feel better. It is a grounding crystal (see page 85). This crystal is good for your intuition (see page 35) and helps you meditate by keeping you focused.

It's good for your knees, ankles, hands, fingers, wrists, feet, and legs.

Bronzite

● **CHAKRA:** heart

This is usually found as a brown rock with gold flakes inside it. It comes from Brazil.

HOW IT HELPS: Bronzite gives you confidence and courage to do all the things you want to do.

Rutilated quartz

● ● **CHAKRA:** brow and crown

This is a quartz crystal with silver or golden threads of another crystal called rutile growing through it. It comes from Brazil, where it's known as angel hair crystal.

HOW IT HELPS: This crystal is very helpful if you're feeling sad. It boosts your energy and gives you confidence, so you can cope with whatever is making you sad and be happy again. It's calming if you feel anxious.

It can help keep you well and make you better if you get hurt.

Crystals with crystals inside them

Some crystals, like rutilated quartz (above) and tourmalinated quartz (see page 103), can have other crystals growing inside them which make them special.

Crazy lace agate

● **CHAKRA:** heart

This is a type of agate (see page 83) with "crazy" patterns of bands and wavy lines in brown, red, and cream colors. It comes from Mexico.

HOW IT HELPS: This crystal gives you lots of confidence, so it helps if you feel shy when you meet new friends. It makes you feel better about yourself and gives you courage to try new things.

It's good for your speech and eyesight. Crazy lace agate crystal washing water (see page 48) helps your skin, and it brings inner strength and positivity, allowing you to shine in every way.

Petrified wood

● **CHAKRA:** base

This is made from old trees that lived a long time ago when there were dinosaurs. After the trees died, they turned into stone. It's found worldwide, especially in Madagascar and the USA.

HOW IT HELPS: Petrified wood is a calming stone and helpful if you feel worried or anxious. It is grounding (see page 85) and helps you connect with nature when you're out in the woods, at the park, or in your garden. It even helps you connect to the natural energy of a pot plant or window box with flowers or herbs growing in it.

It's good for allergies, like hay fever, and your bones.

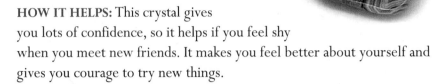

Aragonite

● **CHAKRA:** crown

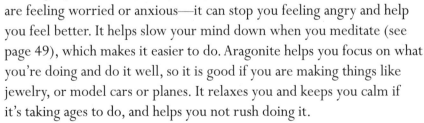

This crystal is hexagon-shaped (see page 16) and can look like a "sputnik," which is a Russian spaceship from the 1960s. It comes from Morocco and Namibia.

HOW IT HELPS: This is a good, calming crystal to have with you if you are feeling worried or anxious—it can stop you feeling angry and help you feel better. It helps slow your mind down when you meditate (see page 49), which makes it easier to do. Aragonite helps you focus on what you're doing and do it well, so it is good if you are making things like jewelry, or model cars or planes. It relaxes you and keeps you calm if it's taking ages to do, and helps you not rush doing it.

Aragonite crystal washing water (see page 48) is good for your hair and can help if your muscles ache or you have skin conditions, like eczema or psoriasis.

RAINBOW

These are more than one color in the same stone and help you be the best you can be.

Rainbow moonstone

● CHAKRA: sacral

This moonstone (see page 81) is a white stone with blue to rainbow-colored flashes, which comes from India.

HOW IT HELPS: This crystal can calm you if you're feeling worried, soothe you if you're upset, and focus your mind. It helps you to help other children and parents feel better. When there are changes and new beginnings happening, like starting a new school or moving home, it gives you confidence. It's a happy stone.

Rainbow moonstone crystal washing water (see page 48) is good for your skin and hair.

Rainbow fluorite

● CHAKRA: brow

This rainbow-colored fluorite (see page 83) comes from China.

HOW IT HELPS: This crystal focuses your thoughts so you can do well in tests, sports, and competitions, even if you're worried. It helps to keep you well, too.

Titanium quartz

● ● ● ● ● ● ●

CHAKRA: all chakras

This amazing rainbow-colored crystal is made of quartz mixed together with special minerals (see page 10) called titanium and niobium. It comes from the USA.

HOW IT HELPS: Titanium quartz makes you feel better about everything! It reassures you when things around you are changing, like moving home or changing schools. It can give you a boost of energy if you're feeling tired. It is useful if you're thinking about what you want to do when you grow up. Titanium quartz helps you to meditate (see page 49) and feel crystal energy (see page 30), so you can sense the energy through touch in your hands and maybe even see, smell, and hear it.

It is good to keep near you if you have a fever, and can help to keep you well.

Peacock ore

● **CHAKRA:** crown

This is a bright, colorful rock from Mexico which can be gold, blue, green, and purple. The color comes from a very thin natural layer on the surface, so scratching it may remove the bright colors, leaving a gray rock. It should not be put into water (see page 41).

HOW IT HELPS: Peacock ore helps you join in doing things with your friends, say what you're thinking, and have fun and be happy. Peacock ore is good for meditation (see page 49) and mindfulness (see page 53), helping you to focus on what you are doing without distraction.

It's good for your tummy.

Labradorite

● **CHAKRA:** crown

This is a gray-green rock with brilliant, bright flashes of blue, red, gold, and green. These colors happen because light bounces around inside the crystal and makes the different colors that you can see. This crystal can be found in Canada, Madagascar, and Norway.

HOW IT HELPS: This makes magic happen around you, like Harry Potter's magic wand—when you have labradorite, good things seem to happen all by themselves! It's good for meditation (see page 49) because it focuses your mind. It helps creativity, like drawing or painting colorful pictures. It is calming if you're feeling worried or anxious.

Labradorite is good for your tummy and eyes.

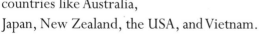

Abalone shell

● **CHAKRA:** throat

This comes from a seashell with brilliant colors inside, which is found in oceans around the world and countries like Australia, Japan, New Zealand, the USA, and Vietnam.

HOW IT HELPS: It helps you feel calm if you are worried or anxious. If you're scared, upset, or angry, it can soothe you.

It's good for your eyes and helps you see the beautiful, colorful things in nature around you.

Angel aura quartz

● ● ● ● ● ● ●
CHAKRA: all chakras

This is a quartz crystal mixed together with special minerals (see page 10) called platinum and silver, making beautiful rainbow crystals with gentle colors and gentle energy. It comes from the USA.

HOW IT HELPS: Angel aura quartz helps you find your guardian angel, who will help you if you feel worried, anxious, or sad. It helps you to care for nature and the environment.

It is a good crystal to keep you well.

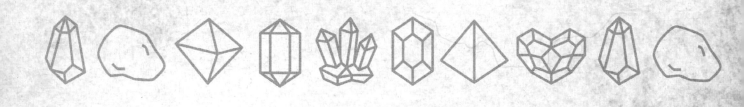

CHAPTER 6

How can my crystals help me?

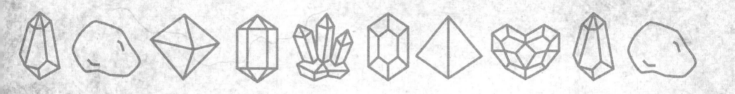

There are lots of different crystals that can help make your day brighter, easier, and happier. This chapter shows you which crystals can help you if you're not feeling great.

Finding a crystal to help you

If you want your crystals to help you with something, like if you're feeling worried, have big changes around you, or simply want to make things better, this chapter will show you the crystals you need, and will also tell you what you need to do with them. But when you're in any place and need help from your crystal friends, remember SBIS (see page 53).

 is for STOP

 is for BREATHE

 is for IMAGINE

 is for SMILE

If you're anxious or worried

There are lots of crystals that can help you feel better about whatever is bothering you. Whenever you feel worried, pick up the closest crystal to you and SBIS (see page 53) for an instant effect!

To help you sleep better

If you aren't sleeping very well, put any of these crystals on your nightstand, hold one of them when you go to sleep, or put one under your pillow:

- Amethyst
- Blue calcite
- Celestite
- Falcon's eye
- Hematite
- Lapis lazuli
- Peach aventurine
- Smoky quartz
- Sodalite
- Strawberry quartz

You can also try the Sleep Well meditation on page 61.

Other ways to sleep better with crystals

• If you have nightmares, put amethyst, flint, or smoky quartz under your pillow, or blue calcite, celestite, or smoky quartz next to your bed on your nightstand.

• For lovely dreams, put amethyst, jade, or smoky quartz under your pillow or on your nightstand.

• To remember your dreams, put amethyst, blue calcite, celestite, kyanite, lapis lazuli, red jasper, or spirit quartz under your pillow or on your nightstand.

• To make your dreams come true, put amber and howlite under your pillow to help.

Amethyst

Blue calcite

Celestite

To feel calm and relaxed

If you're anxious about things like school or your friends, then choose one crystal from this list of calming crystal friends to keep with you all the time so you can SBIS (see page 53) whenever you need to.

- Abalone shell
- Amazonite
- Amethyst
- Angel aura quartz
- Aquamarine
- Aragonite
- Black tourmaline
- Blue calcite
- Blue lace agate
- Celestite
- Chrysocolla
- Dalmatian stone
- Fluorite
- Green aventurine
- Harlequin quartz
- Herkimer diamond
- Howlite
- Kyanite
- Labradorite
- Lapis lazuli
- Lepidolite
- Morganite
- Orange selenite
- Peridot
- Petrified wood
- Pink opal
- Red calcite
- Rose quartz
- Shungite
- Snowflake obsidian
- Strawberry quartz
- Tourmalinated quartz
- Tree agate

You can hold any of these crystals, wear them as jewelry, or put them under your pillow or next to your bed at night. You can also put them in your schoolbag, so you have them nearby during the day.

Other crystals that can help you feel calm

- Jet gives you calmness and positive energy.

- You can put amber in your bath to turn the water into crystal washing water (see page 48), which is very relaxing.

- You can put larger crystals, such as blue calcite, green calcite, or harlequin quartz, in your room so it feels more relaxing and calm when you come home from school, and also next to where you sit in the living room, too.

- If you are worrying a lot about schoolwork or anything to do with your friends, then sunstone, tiger's eye, and turquoise can help you feel better.

If you're panicking

If you're feeling panicky, green calcite is best for you to hold to take away the feeling. But if you're having a panic attack, then green calcite, red calcite, harlequin quartz, or yellow quartz will help you feel calmer. If you get panic attacks often, then you can keep any of these crystals with you to help you stop them.

Green calcite

If you're feeling nervous

If you are nervous about something like being in the school play or in a sports team for a big game, there are four magical crystals to help you feel calmer.

• Golden calcite helps you feel sparkly inside.

• White moonstone is good if you're worried about starting something new.

• Tangerine quartz helps you have fun with your friends.

• Yellow quartz can calm your mind if there are lots of busy things going on inside your head.

Golden calcite

White moonstone

Tangerine quartz

Yellow quartz

If you're feeling afraid

If you're feeling afraid of something, use SBIS (see page 53) and any of these crystals:

• Citrine
• Falcon's eye
• Golden healer quartz
• Rose quartz
• Sodalite
• Tiger's eye

For an extra boost of courage, keep one or more of these crystals in your pocket or schoolbag so they're with you during the day.

Other crystals if you're afraid

• If you need to be brave about something, try bloodstone, bronzite, crazy lace agate, hematite, jade, pink tourmaline, rhodochrosite, sugilite, or turquoise.

• If you need courage to say how you're feeling, aquamarine and carnelian are really good.

• Strawberry aventurine and sunstone will help you to feel strong inside.

• If you're being bullied at school, please tell your parents or teacher.

At school

Calcite is a wonderful crystal to help you with anything to do with going to or being at school, so keep it in your schoolbag so it's with you whenever you need to SBIS (see page 53). It really helps you with learning and is good for any anxiety and worry you may have. It also helps with any kind of reading.

Red calcite

For tests

If you're feeling worried and anxious about tests, there are four special crystals that can help you.

• Green aventurine is very calming if you're feeling worried, and relaxes your muscles, too. It helps you to breathe better if you're breathing fast because you're nervous about a test or something that you don't want to do, like standing up and talking in class.

• Amazonite is a crystal that helps you feel calm if you're nervous, anxious, or worried about tests, as well as about homework or anything else at school or home.

• Fluorite will help you focus in class on your schoolwork so you learn everything you need for your tests.

• Snow quartz helps you have a clear, calm mind and takes away worrying thoughts so you can think about nice things instead.

These crystals are very powerful and magical when you keep them together. Keep them in your schoolbag and hold them when you need to, or imagine having them with you. You can also put them in a small bag in your pocket to keep them safe and take them out of the bag at night and put them on your nightstand. You may like to hold them in your hand when you sleep, or put them under your pillow. Remember to look for them in the morning, as they may be hiding!

Green aventurine

Amazonite

Fluorite

Snow quartz

To help with schoolwork
• Try aquamarine, black tourmaline, carnelian, citrine, Dalmatian stone, lepidolite, tiger's eye, or turquoise. When you're doing your schoolwork at home, put these crystals on your desk or table. Keep them in your pocket or schoolbag when you're at school.

• If you have a test, keep amazonite, aventurine, howlite, orange selenite, rainbow fluorite, rhodonite, or snow quartz close by.

• If you're learning something new, try aquamarine, calcite, citrine, howlite, lepidolite, orange selenite, or purple fluorite.

• When you find it hard to focus on something at school, hold charoite or red calcite, or keep a larger piece of harlequin quartz near you.

• To help you remember things, like things you need to learn for tests or not forgetting to take your lunch to school with you, try amber, apophyllite, hematite, Herkimer diamond, howlite, orange selenite, rhodochrosite, or rhodonite.

• When you're writing stories, calcite, celestite, citrine, rose quartz, and turquoise all help you think of ideas.

• If you have dyslexia, keep a piece of black tourmaline or sugilite with you.

• When you need to do the best you can, hold green aventurine.

Be more creative

Hold any of these crystals and SBIS (see page 53) before you start any creative project, like painting or making a model car. If you get stuck when you're doing it, SBIS again!

• Amazonite
• Black obsidian
• Black tourmaline
• Celestite
• Chrysocolla
• Chrysoprase
• Garnet
• Green aventurine
• Green tourmaline
• Labradorite
• Pink banded agate
• Pyrite
• Rose quartz
• Sodalite

When you're doing art
If you're painting, drawing pictures, or making things, put calcite or rose quartz next to you to help you make them as pretty as they can be.

Feel confident

Keep any of these crystals with you all the time and hold it for an extra boost of confidence when you need it.

- Angelite
- Apache tear
- Black onyx
- Bronzite
- Chrysoprase
- Citrine
- Crazy lace agate
- Golden calcite
- Jade
- Kunzite

- Lodestone
- Peach aventurine
- Pink tourmaline
- Rainbow moonstone
- Rhodonite
- Rose quartz
- Rutilated quartz
- Sodalite
- Strawberry aventurine
- Sugilite

- Tangerine quartz
- Tourmaline
- White moonstone
- Yellow quartz

You can also try the Crystal of Confidence meditation on pages 54–55.

Turquoise

Sodalite

Blue lace agate

For confidence when speaking

- To help you speak in front of others, like your class at school or family, hold amethyst, blue lace agate, or turquoise.

- To feel confident when talking to adults, hold blue lace agate, howlite, or kunzite.

- When there are things you find too embarrassing or difficult to say, hold crazy lace agate, peacock ore, rubellite, or turquoise.

- To say how you feel, hold blue chalcedony, blue lace agate, celestite, golden calcite, harlequin quartz, howlite, kyanite, lapis lazuli, smoky quartz, sodalite, or turquoise.

Change

Whatever is changing, there's a crystal to help you. You can wear any of these crystals, or put them in your pocket or schoolbag, to ease any changes.

- Amethyst
- Apache tear
- Lepidolite
- Moonstone
- Orange selenite
- Tourmaline

Other crystals for change

- If you're starting a new school, amethyst, apache tear, Herkimer diamond, and rainbow moonstone can help you get used to it.

- For really big changes, such as moving home to a new city (or even starting a new school if it feels like a huge change for you), black banded agate is good.

- If lots of things are all changing at the same time, then titanium quartz is helpful to keep near you.

- If you're doing new things, such as going to a new after-school club, keep some of these crystals nearby: citrine, crazy lace agate, lepidolite, orange selenite, pink tourmaline, spirit quartz, and white moonstone.

- If you need to be patient about something, hold aragonite.

Lepidolite

Black banded agate

Aragonite

Difficult thoughts and feelings

Your crystals can help you manage your feelings and emotions, and all the thoughts in your head.

If you're feeling angry

Hold any of these crystals, use SBIS (see page 53), and feel your anger disappear:

- Abalone shell
- Amethyst
- Angelite
- Aquamarine
- Aragonite
- Bloodstone
- Carnelian
- Chalcedony
- Chrysocolla
- Citrine

- Garnet
- Howlite
- Moonstone
- Orange selenite
- Peridot
- Rose quartz
- Smoky quartz
- Snowflake obsidian
- Sugilite

Everyone finds one of these crystals works really well for them, but not necessarily the same one. So your friend might find the crystal that helps them let go of their anger is different from the one that helps you.

If you're having arguments

- If you're having arguments at school or with your friends, carry morganite with you in your pocket or schoolbag.

- If you have arguments at home, put small strawberry aventurine stones around your house to help make things better. (Check with an adult that this is okay.)

- If you need to forgive someone, hold apache tear, moonstone, purple chalcedony, rose quartz, sugilite, or tangerine quartz.

- If you're upset by something a friend says or does, try holding a pink tourmaline and SBIS (see page 53).

Strawberry aventurine

Pink tourmaline

If your mind is full of thoughts

• If you're always thinking of lots of different things, hold yellow quartz and SBIS (see page 53) or put it under your pillow at night to calm your mind down.

• If it feels like your mind is clogged up with too many thoughts, hold snow quartz and SBIS to help clear your mind.

• If you're thinking bad things and the thoughts won't go away, hold tiger's eye and SBIS.

• If you keep getting distracted from what you are doing, hold chrysoprase, Dalmatian stone, red calcite, or sodalite to help you concentrate.

• If you're confused, hold chrysoprase, lodestone, pink opal, or sodalite.

• If you're finding it difficult to make your mind up about something, like which games to play or food to eat, hold amethyst, citrine, fluorite, green aventurine, or peach aventurine to help you decide.

• If you are meditating (see page 49), hold aquamarine, fluorite, peach aventurine, rainbow moonstone, rhodonite, tourmaline, or yellow quartz to focus your mind on the meditation.

Pink opal   **Chrysoprase**

If you're sad

If you want to feel happier, hold or wear any of these crystals:

• Amazonite
• Aqua aura
• Aragonite
• Black tourmaline
• Calcite
• Carnelian
• Garnet
• Golden healer quartz
• Gray banded agate

• Lapis lazuli
• Quartz
• Pink banded agate
• Rhodonite
• Tree agate
• Turquoise
• Smoky quartz
• Spirit quartz

And if you need to bring more happiness into your home, put moonstones in all the rooms. (Check with an adult that this is okay.)

You can also try the Happiness and Sunshine Meditation on pages 25–26.

Friends

In Chapter 4 we found out ways to share your crystals with your friends, but here are other ways that crystals can help your friendships.

To make new friends

These are crystals that can help you make new friends if you go to a new school club or do a new sport. Put one of these in your pocket and keep it with you:

Citrine

- Citrine
- Crazy lace agate
- Dalmatian stone
- Falcon's eye
- Harlequin quartz
- Kunzite
- Moonstone
- Pink tourmaline
- Rose quartz
- Sodalite
- Spirit quartz
- Tangerine quartz
- Turquoise
- White moonstone

If you're missing a special friend

To help you feel better when you miss your friend, at night, keep tourmaline by your bed or hold it while you sleep, and during the day, keep it in your pocket and hold it when you especially miss them.

To bring happiness to you and your friends

Hold or wear any of these crystals:

- Apache tear
- Aqua aura
- Citrine
- Herkimer diamond
- Orange calcite
- Peacock ore
- Peridot
- Pink banded agate
- Rainbow moonstone
- Rhodochrosite
- Rose quartz
- Tourmalinated quartz
- White moonstone

You can also try the Magical Journey meditation on pages 73–75.

Apache tear

To have more fun

Share some of these crystals with your friends and you'll all have more fun:

- Red jasper
- Orange calcite
- Peacock ore
- Rhodochrosite
- Tangerine quartz
- Yellow quartz

Red jasper

Other crystals for fun

• If you're playing games, or chatting with a friend or group of friends in person, on the phone, or online, carnelian, Dalmatian stone, green aventurine, and tiger's eye can help you all have even more fun.

• If you want to laugh more, put tangerine quartz or orange calcite crystal near you, or hold one of them.

• Have fun by doing SBIS (see page 53) too: Stop. Breathe. Imagine you're laughing until you start to giggle out loud. Smile.

Tiger's eye

Boost your energy

If you're feeling tired, hold any of the crystals below. If you tend to get tired at times during the day, keep the crystal with you all day.

- Carnelian
- Dalmatian stone
- Garnet
- Harlequin quartz
- Herkimer diamond
- Pyrite
- Rubellite
- Rutilated quartz
- Smoky quartz
- Sodalite
- Sunstone
- Tangerine quartz
- Titanium quartz
- White moonstone
- Yellow jasper
- Yellow quartz
- Zebra rock

To balance your energy

If you have lots of energy one minute and feel really tired the next, keep kyanite in your pocket during the day to feel better.

Kyanite

Chakra body template

Trace or photocopy this template for Stick the Chakra on the Yogi (see page 38).

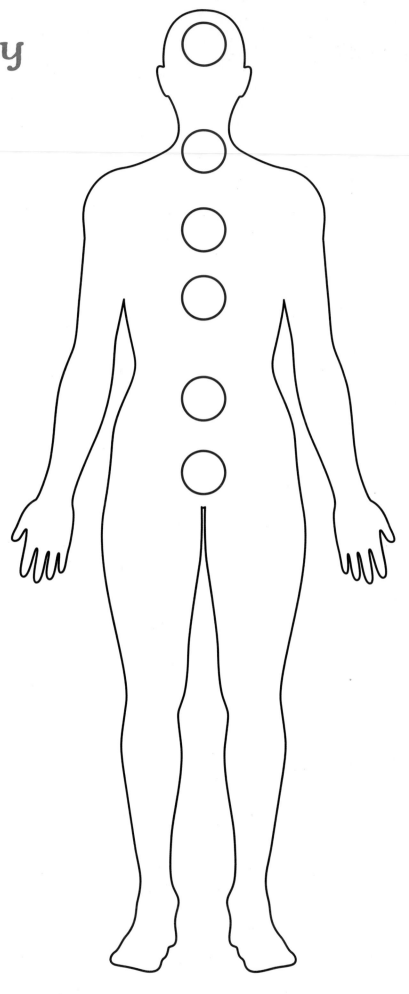

Index

Thank you

A crystal poem

Crystals come in all shapes
and sizes

They're sparkly and shiny and
lovely surprises

They can be round and square,
and heart-shaped, too

And they can help you feel better
if you're feeling sad and blue

There are so many colors,
from purple to pink

It will be exciting to choose the ones
that you think

You'll feel like a magician choosing
one or more

And you'll know it's right because
your intuition will be like a light
opening a door

When you use your pendulum,
it will tell you yes or no

It will give you the crystal you need
and can get to know

You can be calm and relaxed,
breathing in and out

And meditate daily so you won't
want to shout

They're magic and special and
so much fun too

All your worries and upsets will go
and you'll feel like a new happy you

Crystals are special and will protect
you and more

They'll be with you for always
for you to adore

We would like to thank Nicci's amazing daughter-in-law Emma Sandzer, who is a brilliant teacher and gives so much to the seven- to eight-year-old children in her classes. You are such an inspiration, and we appreciate you getting into the minds of your pupils when reading the draft of our book and giving us your feedback. Thank you to Cindy Richards for your patience with this project—which we first talked about in 2006! Carmel Edmonds, thank you for your wise editorial input, as well as all the other people at CICO Books who bring life to our words. Thanks also to the fantastic models—Jasper, Red, Minnie, Lula, and Indi. A magical mention for our amazing puppy Teddy, who brings so much laughter, healing, and happiness to everyone he meets.

From Nicci: I would also like to thank my son Adam, daughter Gemma, son-in-law Adam, and my wonderful parents and family for their continued support and belief in all I do. Thank you to all my fabulous supportive friends. You know who you are! My special thank you goes to my adorable grandson Louis, who is a beautiful shining light. From the age of two, he knew the crystals he loved and has his own special bowl of crystals that he asks to cleanse every week with water and bubbles!

From Philip: I would like to thank my superstar great-nephew Jasper for the way he beautifully modeled our crystals. And the people who inspired me to write—my father Cyril, Melody, all my clients and students, and Ian, who knows why.

Picture credits